"Biblical scholars often compl   ⌐in
about biblical scholars. What i   v?
Who better than Scot McKi   :d,
McKnight winsomely speaks   :al
scholars want them to know   ol-
laboration with our theologian menus. manny jou, scot, for ng
and to-the-point analysis."

Tremper Longman III, distinguished scholar and professor emeritus of biblical studies, Westmont College

"Can't you two get along? The Bible scholar and systematician, fists swinging, are siblings that love to hate each other. Not only does this book show how biblical scholarship and theology serve complementary aims, it also highlights the best of recent integrative scholarship. Scot McKnight has delivered a knockout."

Matthew W. Bates, author of *Salvation by Allegiance Alone* and associate professor of theology at Quincy University

"It is greatly encouraging to see scholars bridging the divide between biblical scholars and systematic theologians, as this will only benefit us all in the long run. In this latest volume, Scot McKnight generously and irenically pushes systematic theologians to pay attention to some oft-neglected themes: Scripture itself, exegesis and historical context, narrative, and lived theologies. His is a fair and even-handed appraisal, even giving credit where credit is due to the value of systematics! This volume will be useful for professors and students alike and, happily, will further the pursuit of interdisciplinary engagement."

Lucy Peppiatt, principal of Westminster Theological Centre, United Kingdom, and author of *Rediscovering Scripture's Vision for Women*

"Like siblings who were separated by divorced parents, biblical studies and theology already have much in common but also need to reacquaint themselves with one another. Addressing key issues and key voices, Scot McKnight helps foster a much-needed reconciliation between these two disciplines that often speak in different ways and value different evidence for their conclusions. This conversation is necessary for the vitality of the church and the academy."

Ben C. Blackwell, associate professor of early Christianity at Houston Theological Seminary

"In the contest of exegesis versus theology, this book offers a way out of methodological shortcomings in both disciplines. Scot's approach unites theological transcendence with historical exegesis and expounds the primacy of Scripture in the context of the church's tradition. Scot is one of the few New Testament scholars who is also conversant in historical theology. Protestant, Catholic, and Orthodox readers will find this book to be wise, insightful, and pioneering."

Bradley Nassif, professor of biblical and theological studies at North Park University

"This book (and its companion) provides a fascinating insight into theology and biblical studies. In his conversation with theologians, McKnight not only raises important methodological questions but also surveys the field of biblical studies and offers some prospects for its future—making this an important read for theologians and biblical scholars alike."

Madison N. Pierce, assistant professor of New Testament at Trinity Evangelical Divinity School

"We modern biblical scholars and theologians tend to work away in our separate silos, wishing 'the other team' respected and employed our work as much as we think they should. There are a few important projects that bring some of us together from time to time, but the kind of honest conversation promoted here is generally hard to find. Scot McKnight doesn't presume to provide us with the last word or even the penultimate word for the dialogue. But this is a very important contribution toward generating the ongoing conversation that will benefit not only biblical scholars and theologians but, most importantly, the church and its mission."

Roy E. Ciampa, S. Louis and Ann W. Armstrong Chair of Religion and chair of the Department of Biblical and Religious Studies, Samford University

"While biblical and theological studies are like separate tribes, each with its own language, rules, and culture, Scot McKnight begins a friendly conversation with theologians from the biblical studies side, showing how theologians can use the Bible more helpfully in their discipline and contribute positively to his world of biblical studies. McKnight's advice to theologians will hopefully be heard and heeded and contribute to breaking down the self-enclosed silos of divinity studies. This book, combined with the sister volume by Hans Boersma, makes for a great conversation."

Michael F. Bird, academic dean and lecturer in theology at Ridley College in Melbourne, Australia

"Thankfully, we live in a day when many theologians want to read the Bible carefully and do theology biblically and when many biblical scholars want to read the Bible theologically and do theology carefully. We need to listen to one another with clarity of sight and charity of affection. This book can help us listen better, and we all may benefit from it."

Thomas H. McCall, Tennent Professor of Theology at Asbury Theological Seminary

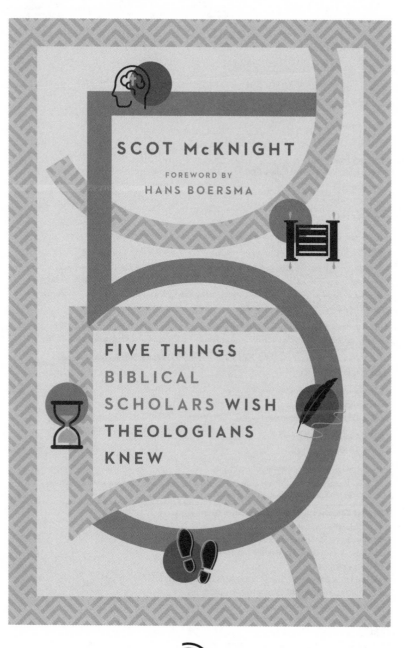

SCOT McKNIGHT

FOREWORD BY
HANS BOERSMA

FIVE THINGS
BIBLICAL
SCHOLARS WISH
THEOLOGIANS
KNEW

IVP
Academic
An imprint of InterVarsity Press
Downers Grove, Illinois

InterVarsity Press
P.O. Box 1400, Downers Grove, IL 60515-1426
ivpress.com
email@ivpress.com

InterVarsity Press® is the book-publishing division of InterVarsity Christian Fellowship/USA®, a movement of students and faculty active on campus at hundreds of universities, colleges, and schools of nursing in the United States of America, and a member movement of the International Fellowship of Evangelical Students. For information about local and regional activities, visit intervarsity.org.

Scripture quotations, unless otherwise noted, are from the New Revised Standard Version Bible, copyright © 1989 National Council of the Churches of Christ in the United States of America. Used by permission. All rights reserved worldwide.

The publisher cannot verify the accuracy or functionality of website URLs used in this book beyond the date of publication.

Cover design and image composite: David Fassett
Interior design: Jeanna Wiggins
Image: art deco texture: © supermimicry / iStock / Getty Images

ISBN 978-0-8308-4935-2 (print)
ISBN 978-0-8308-5517-9 (digital)

Printed in the United States of America ∞

InterVarsity Press is committed to ecological stewardship and to the conservation of natural resources in all our operations. This book was printed using sustainably sourced paper.

Library of Congress Cataloging-in-Publication Data
Names: McKnight, Scot, author.
Title: Five things biblical scholars wish theologians knew / Scot McKnight.
Description: Downers Grove, IL : InterVarsity Press, [2021] | Includes
  bibliographical references.
Identifiers: LCCN 2021012997 (print) | LCCN 2021012998 (ebook) | ISBN
  9780830849352 (print) | ISBN 9780830855179 (digital)
Subjects: LCSH: Theology. | Bible—Criticism, interpretation, etc.
Classification: LCC BR118 .M295 2021 (print) | LCC BR118 (ebook) | DDC
  230—dc23
LC record available at https://lccn.loc.gov/2021012997
LC ebook record available at https://lccn.loc.gov/2021012998

P 25 24 23 22 21 20 19 18 17 16 15 14 13 12 11 10 9 8 7 6 5 4 3 2 1

Y 42 41 40 39 38 37 36 35 34 33 32 31 30 29 28 27 26 25 24 23 22 21

For Brad and Barb Nassif

To know God is unlike any other knowledge;
indeed, it is more truly to be known, and so transformed.

SARAH COAKLEY, GOD, SEXUALITY, AND THE SELF

The churches most faithful to Scripture are not those that legislate
the most honorific propositions about Scripture but those that most often
and thoughtfully read and hear it. . . . The primary doctrine of Scripture
may be stated: privilege *this book within the church's living discourse.*

ROBERT JENSON, SYSTEMATIC THEOLOGY

The canonicity of Scripture and the
catholicity of the church imply each other.

KEVIN VANHOOZER AND DANIEL TREIER,
THEOLOGY AND THE MIRROR OF SCRIPTURE

What then do theologians do? As pastors, they think deeply
and compassionately. As prophets, they think deeply and courageously.
As poets, they think deeply and creatively. Pastors, prophets and poets,
and always in a way that is compassionate, courageous and creative.

BRIAN HARRIS, "WHAT DO THEOLOGIANS DO?"

CONTENTS

FOREWORD

Hans Boersma

I AM JEALOUS OF SCOT MCKNIGHT. I wish I was as up to date on biblical scholarship as he is on dogmatic theology. Scot has closely read John Calvin, Robert Jenson, Fleming Rutledge, Sarah Coakley, Katherine Sonderegger, Beth Felker Jones, Kevin Vanhoozer, and many other theologians. In fact, it's no false humility when I say I wish I had delved as deeply into some of these dogmatic theologians as Scot has. For this reason alone, I couldn't wish for a better dialogue partner than Scot McKnight: he is a biblical theologian thoroughly at home in that "other world" of dogmatic or systematic theology.

True, Scot regularly admits that he both loves and is irritated by some of the dogmatic theologians he reads. This shouldn't surprise us. His book is not about what he wishes biblical scholars knew but about what he wishes theologians knew. His last two chapters make clear that Scot is passionate about his wish that theologians knew more about narrative and about ethics than they typically do. Scot and I may not quite see eye to eye on these topics. But no matter my questions, let me here simply acknowledge that I think the focus of Scot's critique is bang on. He is right to put into question the "soterian gospel" of North American evangelicalism—a decisionist focus on conversion and an individualist view of salvation.

If there's one topic Scot and I might discuss over a beer at the pub one night, it is the Scripture-tradition relationship. Scot discusses tradition mostly when dealing with what he terms the *retrieval model* versus the *expansive model* of interpretation. The former wants to retrieve our theology straight from the Bible, while the latter insists on theological progress and growth in biblical interpretation. The expansive model wants to acknowledge tradition in developing ever-new insights into the biblical text over time. Scot wants to blend key aspects of both models, but it is clear that he is hardly tempted by a strict retrieval model. He rejects a *nuda Scriptura* approach that brackets off the tradition in theological articulation. Scot is not a primitivist or biblicist—in the sense of trying simply to retrieve the original meaning of the text. He is keenly aware that Scripture is meant to be read through the lens of the church's tradition.

Perhaps, after a beer or two, I might dare ask: "Scot, you're talking about how we need tradition for biblical interpretation, and you know I agree. But you also talk repeatedly about taking the Bible as our starting point and about mirroring the Bible's own language and approach. But isn't Scripture itself the outcome of tradition? And if so, doesn't this priority of tradition over Scripture have implications for how we read the Bible?" What I mean is this: long before the church canonized the Scriptures, she had a lived theology in liturgy, creeds, and numerous practices. Yves Congar's *The Meaning of Tradition* draws attention to the importance of this precanonical tradition, pointing out that we would not even have had a "formal teaching on the Eucharist by the apostle Paul, if errors and abuses had not existed in the community of Corinth." Without the life of the church, we would not have the Scriptures themselves.

Why does any of this matter? The reason, I think is this: if Scripture is one of the key elements *of* the tradition, then the church's tradition is the primary (and authoritative) context for biblical reading. Whatever other contexts may shape us—race, color, gender, economic status—these are not part of sacred tradition. That is to say, these experiential factors carry no authority in the practice of exegesis. Only the church's tradition does, for it is only of the church's tradition that we can say it was the womb that gave birth to Holy Scripture. I suppose what makes me skittish about *sola Scriptura*—even McKnight's nuanced version of it—is that with the *sola* approach, it's easy for exhilarating and liberating human experiences to determine whether a particular interpretation is acceptable or not. Put differently, once we let go of the erroneous notion that exegesis is strictly about retrieving the author's original intent, we need to face another question head-on: Which context (or which tradition) shapes our exegetical practices?

Let me be crystal clear: Scot's interpretation of the Bible is theological in character. What is more, he unapologetically insists that theology should be done within the church and ought to have the Great Tradition and the Nicene Creed as its starting point. To admit to a dogmatic lens in reading Scripture is not a source of embarrassment but is, on Scot's understanding, an inescapable aspect of all proper exegesis. Biblical interpretation cannot bracket—let alone leave behind—its basic christological and trinitarian creedal claims. One arrives at a proper reading of the biblical text not despite but in grateful dependence on one's prior creedal convictions. On Scot's understanding, we need a retrieval of patristic modes of interpretation in order to uphold the trinitarian faith and the biblical path by which the early church arrived at it. All of this has my warm endorsement.

What's more, Scot reads the Bible not because he is a historian (though he has many good things to say about the place of history) but as a theologian. His gentle polemic against biblical scholars who see themselves more as historians than as theologians is a breath of fresh air. And this theologian, for one, is grateful for the unambiguous claim that exegesis aims not to find the one, true meaning of the text (authorial intent) but instead seeks the wisdom of knowing God and being known by him. Usually it is dogmatic theologians who quote David Steinmetz's invective against historical criticism as an approach that remains "restricted, as it deserves to be, to the guild and the academy, where the question of truth can be endlessly deferred." It is a delight to read this comment approvingly quoted in the work of a biblical scholar!

More than anything, I am heartened by Scot's unequivocal affirmation that we must read all of Scripture in the light of Christ. Yes, the Christ event is the climax of the biblical narrative, but Scot rightly refuses to treat the Christ event as a later intrusion into an otherwise Christ-less story. Appealing to Robert Jenson's *Systematic Theology*, he insists that the climactic self-revelation of God in Christ ought to shape how we read the entire story, from beginning to end. Once this climactic event happens, writes Scot, it "both gives the narrative its dramatic coherence and sheds light on how to read that narrative." For Scot, this means the Fathers' "spiritual" exegesis was essentially right: the allegorical or christological truth of the narrative lies *within* the narrative itself. In Scot's words: "The Old Testament narrative has futurity written into it." I couldn't agree more. Christ himself is the deeper reality that we look for whenever we read the Old Testament Scriptures. There simply is no deeper ground for agreement between biblical and dogmatic theology than the shared recognition of the real presence of Christ throughout the biblical text.

ACKNOWLEDGMENTS

I AM GRATEFUL TO ANNA GISSING for the invitation and for Hans Boersma for supporting my inclusion in this project. I have long admired Hans's theology and have read his books to great joy.

To my student Ben Davis, for numerous book suggestions. He has also offered feedback that made this book better.

In reading theologians I have routinely written to friends for suggestions and wisdom, including Mike Bird, Lucy Peppiatt, Patrick Mitchel, Jules Martinez, Madison Pierce, Dan Treier, Beth Felker Jones, Geoff Holsclaw, Kevin Vanhoozer, Emily McGowin, Gavin Ortlund, Lynn Cohick, and Matt Bates.

Covid-19's cancellation of all my traveling and speaking engagements opened up time I never imagined I would have for this project. I'm not grateful for the virus, but I do want to record the gloom that the sheltering in place created for all of us as well as express my sadness over the billions who have suffered because of it. "What else am I going to do but work on my writing projects?" I more than once muttered to myself. I am then grateful for the time, not the virus.

INTRODUCTION

So you want to be a theologian? Well, perhaps you answer back, "Not so much a 'systematic' theologian but, yes, a 'theologian.'" You might then suggest, too, that after all, "We are all theologians, and I want to be a good one." I'm glad for you, as I am honored at times to be called a theologian though in my world, and this is what is at the heart of this book and Hans Boersma's companion volume, we Bible scholars tend to call ourselves exegetes or New Testament scholars or, to get a little pedantic, Matthew or John or Paul scholars. People in my discipline, New Testament, sometimes don't like to be called theologians, and at times we (or they) dismiss anything smacking of systematics. Systematic theology is a complete, coherent account of the Christian faith, broken into parts but unified and driven by the system at work. Biblical theology sticks to the Bible and to its categories and terms and limits.

There is, then, to this day often a wide divide between a systematic theologian and a biblical scholar. We don't tend to teach outside our special discipline, and we often don't even read one another. Some days I think there ought to be a required order for doing theology—that is, that we biblical scholars get to go first, and we set the course. That is, we write up our research into an article or a book, lay it on the table in the lunchroom for the faculty, and the systematicians pick it up and work it into their theology. On the best days, I think the systematicians will actually change their theology because of our Bible studies. On other days, I think they mostly ignore us, and (on every day, I suppose) they think we ignore them. We mostly ignore theologians. (Except for Karl Barth.)

Truth be told, many of us in New Testament studies, and even more so those in Old Testament studies, find ourselves fighting off the penchant of students to bring systematics into the discussion in a way that overwhelms the biblical author being studied and redirects the conversation to much later discussions.

> Student: "Professor, Barth put forward this theory of Scripture. Is his view about what David is saying in Psalm 119 right?"

> Professor: "Let David be David and you can discuss Barth in your systematic theology classes."

Theology is more than Barth or any other contemporary theologian. In Professor James D. G. Dunn's much-discussed *Christology in the Making*, a book that investigates the origins of belief in the incarnation and that concludes incarnational Christology is not to be found until the last-written documents of the New Testament, the question of the orthodox creeds comes up in his introduction—that is, theology in its most received form comes up. He writes about pressing questions, observing, "And for those who like myself find the definition of Christianity more clearly provided by the NT than by the creeds of Catholic Christendom the answers to these questions will have a critical bearing on faith itself." This statement is followed by a very common warning by professors of my discipline: "But all should bear in mind that truly to hear the NT writers speaking in their own terms requires that the listener be open to the possibility that some of his preconceived ideas will be challenged and have to be rejected even when others are confirmed."[1] I remember reading this in 1980 as a seminary student and thinking, *A scholar after my own heart.* I'm not where I was those days, but I am convinced that we must begin with the Bible, and we must let the Bible speak on its own, and we must cede to the Bible the categories it provides. But we are getting ahead of ourselves. There you have our problem: Bible versus creeds versus confessions versus systematics. Perhaps not always "versus," but these are the tension points to be explored in this volume and Hans Boersma's *Five Things Theologians Wish Biblical Scholars Knew.*

NEW TESTAMENT SCHOLARS' USE OF SYSTEMATICS

I give two examples of how this plays out, and how it plays out varies considerably. Volker Rabens, a young German New Testament scholar, in his study of the Holy Spirit and ethics and how the Spirit's indwelling transforms, says this about another New Testament scholar: "Stalder's study on sanctification and pneumatology in Paul is heavily influenced by the *topoi* of systematic theology." Before the punch line, notice that he sees the typical categories of systematics to be too influential in this New Testament scholar's work. So? "He will thus not be our main dialogue partner."[2] Rabens, courteously but firmly, puts Stalder's work back on the shelf because it has been too influenced by systematic categories for doing biblical studies.

Now a second example, this one from another New Testament scholar, a preeminent Pauline scholar at Duke Divinity School, Douglas Campbell. At the beginning of his massive volume *Pauline Dogmatics,* he says, "So I suggest that an accurate account of Paul reads him in a quite Barthian way primarily because Barth was in many ways a faithful interpreter of Paul." At the end he says, "I have explicated

[1]James D. G. Dunn, *Christology in the Making: A New Testament into the Origins of the Doctrine of the Incarnation,* 2nd ed. (Philadelphia: Westminster John Knox, 1989), 10.
[2]Volker Rabens, *The Holy Spirit and Ethics in Paul: Transformation and Empowering for Religious-Ethical Life,* 2nd ed. (Minneapolis: Fortress, 2014), 2n5.

Paul with the help of Karl Barth," and, "I am now more firmly convinced than ever that we must begin with Barth." Wow, the word he
uses is *begin*. Begin "with Barth." That's quite a confession for those
of us formed into New Testament studies when bracketing systematics *and* systematicians was the first rule of exegesis. That claim by
Campbell is a stretch for many of us, but what Campbell drops in the
footnote of that same page would be seen as methodologically unac-
ceptable: "If my reader is getting nervous about the emphasis on Barth,
may I point out (again) that Paul is best read as Barthian because
Barth got most of his good stuff *from* Paul. Barth was a Paulinist."[3]
The question could be asked, But was Paul a Barthian?

One scholar shelves with precision someone who makes use of
systematic categories, and one scholar openly contends a systematician is the best way to understand Paul himself. It's not that simple,
perhaps, but nuances will be brought into discussion in the chapters
that follow. We want merely here to put the tension into play. There
is a difference between biblical and systematic theology, between
what Old and New Testament scholars are trained to do and what
systematicians are trained to do.

THE SEDUCTION OF SYSTEMATICS

I speak now as a biblical specialist. Theology in general is seductive
because we are studying God, and this is true for the biblical and the
systematic theologian. Studying God is both thrilling and intoxicating.
Many times we lose sight of the Subject and begin to obsess about
one of the human authors in the Bible, the world of the Bible, the
intricacies of the history that shaped a given theologian, and the cultural context. We become historians rather than worshipers. Long
ago Leon Morris, a highly respected Australian evangelical, argued
the letter to the Romans was about God. That should have shocked

---

[3]Douglas A. Campbell, *Pauline Dogmatics: The Triumph of God's Love* (Grand Rapids, MI:
Eerdmans, 2020), 2, 742-43. The footnote is 743n3.

many interpreters because Morris showed how few studies of Romans said much about God.[4] It was decades before I heard anyone else call attention to the God-shaped theology of Romans, and the one I heard do so was Beverly Gaventa.[5] One would think in reading most discussions about Romans that the letter is about justification or soteriology, but, no, Morris and Gaventa are right: first it's about God in Christ. Talk about God and talk about history tend to be zero-sum games or the inverse of each other: those who talk about God don't talk much history, and those who talk history seem afraid to talk about God.

That topic—God—can be intoxicating in another way: it can be numbing. So, Brian Harris, another Australian (actually South African now living in Perth), can say,

> Theology is a dangerous business. Though we might begin by feeling that we are in control of the process (we study God) we soon discover that the God we study is the God who studies us. Even as we examine the nature and character of God, we sense the pushback, "You think you are studying me—but actually I am studying your response to what you discover. Never forget, those who study God are challenged to live in the light of what they find." It is dangerous to be a theologian and to be resistant to change, for you cannot study God and not change.[6]

The intoxicating power of studying God is the point of the early sections of J. I. Packer's *Knowing God*.[7] The so-called object of theological study is the all-consuming Subject, who interrogates us as the object, and being known by the Subject is the only true theology.

[4]Leon L. Morris, "The Theme of Romans," in *Apostolic History and the Gospel: Biblical and Historical Essays Presented to F. F. Bruce on His 60th Birthday*, ed. W. Ward Gasque and Ralph P. Martin (Grand Rapids, MI: Eerdmans, 1970), 249-63.

[5]Beverly Gaventa, *When in Romans: An Invitation to Linger with the Gospel According to Paul* (Grand Rapids, MI: Baker Academic, 2018), 75-96. Gaventa has said this in numerous places, and it is not unnoticed that she has been heavily influenced by Barth.

[6]Brian Harris, "What Do Theologians Do?," January 8, 2019, https://brianharrisauthor.com/what-do-theologians-do/.

[7]J. I. Packer, *Knowing God*, 20th anniversary ed. (Downers Grove, IL: InterVarsity Press, 1993).

That seduction can be sensed in yet another way: not only is the Subject intoxicating, but the pursuit of that Subject by exploring truth is seductive. I speak as a New Testament specialist, but there are times when I envy the chasing down of new ideas in new contexts with new categories by theologians *in order that they might ascertain truth more clearly and feel it more deeply.* The reading of the great theologians— from the Cappadocians and Augustine to Vladimir Lossky, Jürgen Moltmann, Sarah Coakley, and Katherine Sonderegger—makes one yearn to enter the exhilaration of discoveries. I say this without diminishing what I think is the noble calling of biblical studies, for there too one enters the world of divine communication in order to know the truth.

Seduction, then, works in many directions, and this must be said about systematics (as it is said about biblical studies): the history of the discussion seduces us into thinking that only those in that history matter. Which is to say that diversity is eliminated, erased, or suppressed by entering into that traditional history of theology. While the Eastern Orthodox Church may talk about its Macrina and the Western church about its Teresa of Ávila, a brief mention of a female doesn't the problem solve. Complicate this now by the burgeoning growth of non-American and non-European voices (and this can be said in other ways), and all of us face a very serious challenge to learn to think with others when it comes to theology.[8] Our history of theology's exclusion of such diverse voices makes the intentionality of including other voices all the more important. I know I have often failed at this myself, and I know this book will not remedy those failures completely, but I will make attempts here to listen to more voices. I have in writing this book at times paused to ask myself whether the five points I make are not five white-male topics of discussion.

---

[8]Robert Chao Romero, *Brown Church: Five Centuries of Latina/o Social Justice, Theology, and Identity* (Downers Grove, IL: IVP Academic, 2020).

Another dimension of systematic theology's seductiveness is the clarity—sometimes wrong, sometimes right—of systemic thinking, the clarity of a system of thought that puts it all together. For instance, F. D. E. Schleiermacher considered all talk about future eschatology as not worthy of knowledge, and many today (sadly) have revived the German's theory.[9] Such dismissals lead ministers to lie or offer comforting pablum at funerals. On the other hand, take trinitarian theology: the third and fourth centuries took endless hours and debates and meetings (and deaths) to come to terms with trinitarian thinking, which (as one narrative goes) was less emphatic in the West than in the East. The penetrations of trinitarian theology, according to the standard narrative, got a decisive push in the *Church Dogmatics* of Karl Barth. Since Barth an increasing number of theologians have learned to think trinitarian-ly, including Robert Jenson.[10] Trinitarian thought can itself become intoxicating and seductive. When Jenson discusses the image of God, instead of probing what *tselem* (and *demuth*) meant in the ancient Near East, he explores the idea on top of Barth's relational theory, leading Jenson to see "image of God" as meaning that humans can both be addressed by God and respond to God as well as speak to one another. His discussion is mesmerizing and miles from what biblical scholars have known for decades: that the term refers not so much (if at all) to our capacity to respond to God's word as to our *mission and task to represent God on earth to ensure God's rule is implemented in all creation.* It is not that Jenson's speech-response theory isn't theologically sound or evocative—it is that the expression "image of God" doesn't mean that in its context. His trinitarian

---

[9]Friedrich Schleiermacher, *Christian Faith: A New Translation and Critical Edition*, trans. Edwina Lawler, Terrence N. Tice, and Catherine L. Kelsey, ed. Terrence N. Tice and Catherine L. Kelsey (Louisville, KY: Westminster John Knox, 2016), 2:992-98.

[10]For a lively study of Jenson's theology, see Lincoln Harvey, *Jesus in the Trinity: A Beginner's Guide to the Theology of Robert Jenson* (London: SCM Press, 2020). For a critique of his trinitarian thinking, see Scott R. Swain, *The God of the Gospel: Robert Jenson's Trinitarian Theology* (Downers Grove, IL: IVP Academic, 2013); Katherine Sonderegger, *Systematic Theology: The Doctrine of God*, vol. 1 (Minneapolis: Fortress, 2015).

commitment led him to ask, "How do we explain 'image of God' in terms of Trinity?" and not, "What does this expression mean in this text in its context, and how does that shape theology?"[11] Once one is committed to one's system, one tends to see that system everywhere.

In only a slight twist of meaning to the word, the *seduction* of systematic theology is its ease when compared to the discipline of exegesis and the patience it requires. I'm fully aware, having read theologians for nearly fifty years, of the scholarly apparatus of their disciplines and the intense study required to become a systematician, but my experience is that theology per se comes more naturally and in some ways more easily than does biblical, exegetical theology. Theology can get in the way of hearing the Bible. One can, to put it bluntly, give a theological opinion about most anything, but to give an informed judgment on whether *pistis Christou* is objective or subjective (or a third way) requires the accumulation of a discipline and practice and knowledge. I'm pressing this from my side of the ledger in the contest of exegesis versus theology, but I do so from the experience of teaching students for nearly four decades. If I ask what one's theory of atonement is, many would have a theory. But if I asked for detailed demonstration of their atonement theory from Jesus or Hebrews, they'd mostly draw a blank. If I were to ask what "righteousness of God" means, especially in Isaiah, most would go silent. Theology seems to come earlier than exegetical expertise. Add history along with Jewish, Roman, and Greek contexts to this, and suddenly the playing field becomes too big for many. It's easier to read a theologian —and I truly mean this—than it is to master Hebrew and Aramaic

---

[11]Robert W. Jenson, *Systematic Theology* (New York: Oxford University Press, 1997), 2:53-72. For recent studies see J. Richard Middleton, *The Liberating Image: The Imago Dei in Genesis 1* (Grand Rapids, MI: Brazos, 2005); Ryan S. Peterson, *Imago Dei as Human Identity*, Journal of Theological Interpretation Supplement 14 (Winona Lake, IN: Eisenbrauns, 2016). This is not to say Jenson should have known what was published after his book; Middleton and Peterson summarize much scholarship that could have been appropriated by Jenson. I don't see that Peterson, however, interacted (as he might have) with Jenson's discussion of image of God in *Systematic Theology* 2:53-72.

and Greek, to scour the ancient sources of Judaism and the Greco-Roman world, then to engage two millennia of conversation and debate about each passage in the New Testament, *and then say something fresh.* I'm not saying that theologians are anything but demanding to read and even more to master. My point is that we all operate with a kind of instinctive systematic theology, and it comes first, while the requirement to think exclusively in terms of Matthew or Hebrews forces us out of our instinctive patterns of thought into others that are anything but common in the church. It is hard work for Bible professors to get students to think in terms of the particular author or book of the Bible instead of morphing that author or text into the larger theological and truth questions. What Matthew means by *kingdom* over against what Mark means is simply not a question most young students think (or even care) about. But they may well (and nearly always do) have an opinion of what *kingdom* means. And since they've not studied the texts, they can be surprised by what it meant in Jesus' world.[12]

Speaking with a theologian one day, I told him about this project and then I said, "I've smarted off about this long enough now I should put something down in print." What I have found is that it's easier to take easy swipes at those down the hallway in theology than it is to construct some major ideas that I wish theologians knew or, in most cases, wish were more pervasive in their theologies. I read lots of theologians who I think maintain good balance—such as Beth Felker Jones—but I also see things that make me cringe. This will not be a polemical book but will instead be a meandering through five topics. At times it will pause to offer some criticisms (and not always of theologians). Before I get there, I want to cover some bases: assumptions at work in good theology. I'll mention some of these, albeit very briefly.

---

[12]Scot McKnight, *Kingdom Conspiracy: Returning to the Radical Mission of the Local Church* (Grand Rapids, MI: Brazos, 2014).

ASSUMPTIONS IN A THEOLOGICAL PROJECT

Genuine theology, biblical and systematic, is *a quest to know God,* or to be known by God and in the embrace of being known by God to become more like God's Son through the gracious work of the Spirit. Scripture plays a major role in shaping what we know and how we know, but good theology eventually admits that it must be at some level limited. What we know of God in being known by God is a speck of divine immensity, but we are confident that God has revealed himself (Godself) in Christ as God's Word and in the Scriptures as God's Word about that Word. There is a tendency in some theologians to press what we don't know hard enough that one wonders whether one can know God at all.[13] Hence, I want to drive in a stake: all theology must start at the exegetical level. At times theologians occasionally toss in some Bible references to decorate their theology rather than to let the Bible form their theology. Kevin Vanhoozer and Daniel Treier wisely then speak of the mirror of Scripture in the sense of its primary idiom, and what they mean is that our language needs to mirror the language of the Bible.[14]

All theology is *wisdom.* There is a rich history of wisdom in the Bible, which can't be isolated to the Old Testament's so-called Wisdom books, and that history did not stop with the Bible, as we find it in noncanonical texts as well. Once we recognize that theology is wisdom, the whole Bible becomes wisdom—searching, finding, articulating, living. If we define wisdom as living in God's world in God's way, that is, as Christoformity, then all of theology needs to

---

[13]E.g., Sarah Coakley, *God, Sexuality, and the Self: An Essay "On the Trinity"* (Cambridge: Cambridge University Press, 2013), 45-46. She speaks of "knowing in unknowing." For a similar point, see Benjamin Myers, "Exegetical Mysticism: Scripture, *Paideia,* and the Spiritual Senses," in *Sarah Coakley and the Future of Systematic Theology,* ed. Janice McRandal (Minneapolis: Fortress, 2016), 1-14.

[14]Kevin J. Vanhoozer and Daniel J. Treier, *Theology and the Mirror of Scripture: A Mere Evangelical Account* (Downers Grove, IL: IVP Academic, 2015).

be wrapped up in wisdom. It is unfortunate that both biblical and systematic theologians can turn theology into history or philosophy, and forget that it is about God and about wisdom and knowing God and being known by God. This kind of pursuit of wisdom, then, fears the common practice of bracketing off sources for genuine wisdom. In particular, the Christian faith uniformly confesses a trinitarian God, and that means theology must be trinitarian.

The living embodiment of that wisdom is that theology comes to us from the church, and hence all good theology is *ecclesial*. Yet we live in a divided church, not the church we confess in the creed, and thus our theology becomes partisan, or close to it, the moment we put pen to paper. True enough, but the church is what it is, and that "is-ness" gives shape to genuine Christian theology. Theology is not simply ideas articulated in disinterested fashion but ideas embodied in the context of church life. Which means our theology—and here I will meet some hesitations from those in my own disciplines—needs to be constrained, checked, challenged by the great tradition of the church, and that means beginning with the Nicene Creed. Then, too, our biblical studies at least need to be reshaped and redirected by our own denominational theology. This in part is what I mean by saying theology is ecclesial.

Something Sarah Coakley presses into play often is that all theology is *prayerful*, which she can call ascetical or refer to contemplation, contemplative prayer, and the more solitary spiritual disciplines. While her focus seems to be more individualistic, she's an Anglican, and that means she's at least tipping her hat to the great prayer traditions of the church, including the Book of Common Prayer's collects.[15] Thus, theology is also worshipful and personal as

---

[15] Coakley, *God, Sexuality, and the Self*, 88. For a good explanation of her approach with some of its weaknesses, see Myles Werntz, "The Body and the Body of the Church: Coakley, Yoder, and the Imitation of Christ," in McRandal, *Sarah Coakley and the Future*, 99-114.

well as corporate and ecclesial.[16] What is said about Coakley can be said as well about Katherine Sonderegger's theology: she explodes at times into lyrical worship.[17]

Returning now to something hinted at: all theology is *cultural*. Every theologian speaks out of a culture, into that culture, and for that culture. Theology is located, and that means males and females and ethnic groups and races and ages and denominations are all at work in how theology is formed and embodied. There is no such thing as a theology done once and for all. Unredeemed desire, Coakley reminds us over and over, is behind the hegemonic articulations and embodiments that impede genuine Christian unity in our pursuit of knowing God and being known by God.[18] But theologian John Webster reminds us that theology is not only cultural because it also produces a culture and requires a kind of culture for it to flourish as God's design. I finish this introduction, then, with words from Webster, words that set the tone for the chapters that follow:

> There can be few things more necessary for the renewal of Christian theology than the promotion of awed reading of classical Christian texts, scriptural and other, precisely because a good deal of modern Christian thought has adopted habits of mind which have led to disenchantment with the biblical canon and the traditions of paraphrase and commentary by which the culture of Christian faith has often been sustained. Such practices of reading and interpretation, and the educational and

---

[16]A noticeable weakness in Coakley's first volume is an absence of ecclesiology in her trinitarian ecstasy theory. Does the church desire? For a set of responses to Coakley, see McRandal, *Sarah Coakley and the Future*. On this deficit in ecclesiology, see Werntz, "Body," 105. Her focus on Rom 8 fails to note that in Rom 8 there is an ecclesiology at work (Rom 8:18, in "us"; Rom 8:19, "children of God"; Rom 8:21, "children of God"; Rom 8:23, "we" and "the redemption of our bodies"; Rom 8:24, "we"; Rom 8:27, "saints"; Rom 8:28, in "for those who love God"; of course, Rom 8:29-30). All these indicate the prayer of the Spirit-prompted groaning is an ecclesiological group.
[17]Sonderegger, *Systematic Theology*.
[18]Coakley, *God, Sexuality, and the Self*, 51-52.

political strategies which surround them, are central to the task of creating the conditions for the nurture of Christian theology.[19]

It is because I care about the Bible as God's Word, as sacred Scripture, that I have taken the alternative side to this two-book approach to the questions about what we wish the other one knew. The fundamental starting point is that we Bible folks think systematicians sometimes get a bit too far from Scripture, and so I want to explore five topics that I wish budding theologians would keep in front of them as they do their work: (1) theology needs a constant return to Scripture, (2) theology needs to know its impact on biblical studies, (3) theology needs historically shaped biblical studies, (4) theology needs more narrative, and (5) theology needs to be lived theology.

---

[19]John Webster, *The Culture of Theology*, ed. Ivor J. Davidson and Alden C. McCray (Grand Rapids, MI: Baker Academic, 2019), 45.

THEOLOGY NEEDS A CONSTANT RETURN TO SCRIPTURE

I BEGAN WITH THE OBSERVATION that biblical scholarship and systematic theology differ from each other. We differ at perhaps the deepest level in method. Put in starkly contrasting terms, the former begins with the Bible, and the latter somewhere else. This, from long experience, is a common complaint I have heard among biblical scholars. We think systematicians often impose on the text, while we think we don't, truth be told, or at least we admit we try not to. This is an overstatement, but I want to begin here because this is how we Bible folks (sometimes) talk about systematicians, especially when they are not present.

Bible scholars study books in the Bible, and they do so with some kind of method.[1] Some focus so much on history that the biblical author and the divine Author disappear behind a reconstruction of

---

[1] A good example is Michael J. Gorman, *Elements of Biblical Exegesis*, rev. ed. (Grand Rapids, MI: Baker Academic, 2010).

what happened, while others seek to set the Bible in its historical context in order to elucidate the text itself more accurately. Some are less concerned with history and context and devote themselves to a reconstructed narrative of the Bible as the contextual clue for reading, say, Mark's Gospel. Others are so intent on the grammar and syntax of the text itself that context and narrative are rarely brought into play. These, and no doubt nuances could be added, are all part of what we mean by biblical scholarship.[2]

The recent shift for some toward what A. C. Thiselton comprehensively described as socio-pragmatics (but which today often goes by political or liberation theology) deserves mention for two reasons: (1) it has penetrating value, and (2) it replaces classic systematic theology for its practitioners.[3] Liberationist readings of the Bible, whether from African Americans, Latin Americans, Korean Americans, American Indians, Asians, feminists and womanists and Marxists, take a stand in a given location and read the Bible out of that location and for that location.[4] The singular point so well made by such readings is that each of us stands in a location when we read the Bible. There is no escaping such a feet-in-the-mud approach to Bible reading, nor is there an escape for the sharp angles drawn by such an approach to the Bible. But when one reads the most candid of such approaches—say, what one finds in Gustavo Gutiérrez or Brian Blount or Elsa Támez—one has to ask at times whether the Bible itself is being *used* more than being read, or whether at times such approaches overwhelm what the Bible says, or whether important elements of what the Bible says are being ignored. Once again, we all have contexts and we are all located, but what Bible scholars

---

[2]A more recent sketch of major trends is Markus Bockmuehl, *Seeing the Word: Refocusing New Testament Study*, Studies in Theological Interpretation (Grand Rapids, MI: Baker Academic, 2006), 13-74.

[3]Anthony C. Thiselton, *New Horizons in Hermeneutics* (Grand Rapids, MI: Zondervan, 1992).

[4]Mary M. Veeneman, *Introducing Theological Method: A Survey of Contemporary Theologians and Approaches* (Grand Rapids, MI: Baker Academic, 2017), 111-67.

often want to emphasize is that the Bible *needs to challenge our locations if the Bible is going to do its own work*. This is all a matter of lovingly listening to the text, about which I will say more.[5]

But how does one listen to the text in a loving manner?[6] How does one acquire a reliable, accurate reading of the Bible's own text? How does a biblical scholar contest the approach of the systematician or a political approach to reading the Bible? I suggest two impulses in models for doing theology, simplified in order to draw out of each its distinctive contributions: the retrieval model and the expansive model.[7] These two models are on either end of a spectrum from Bible to greater expansions in theology. The retrieval model tends to resist both systematics and socio-pragmatics, while the expansive model tends to embrace both in unequal measure. When we are finished sketching these two models, I will propose an integrative model that takes what is best from each of the other two models.[8] I can think of very few whose method is not a nuanced combination of both of these impulses. Mary Veeneman's fine textbook on theological method makes this altogether clear.[9]

Following the discussion of models, I will turn to two significant issues in all biblical and theological interpretation: (1) the primacy of turning to Scripture first and (2) the charge of biblicism by those who believe theology must stick to the Bible.

---

[5]Gustavo Gutiérrez, *A Theology of Liberation: History, Politics, and Salvation*, rev. ed. (Maryknoll, NY: Orbis Books, 1988); Gutiérrez, *We Drink from Our Own Wells: The Spiritual Journey of a People* (Maryknoll, NY: Orbis Books, 2010); Brian K. Blount, *Then the Whisper Put on Flesh: New Testament Ethics in an African American Context* (Nashville: Abingdon, 2001); Elsa Támez, *The Scandalous Message of James: Faith Without Works Is Dead*, rev. ed. (New York: Herder & Herder, 2002); Alan Jacobs, *A Theology of Reading: The Hermeneutics of Love* (Boulder, CO: Westview, 2001).

[6]Jacobs, *Theology of Reading*.

[7]A similar set of poles is found in Markus Bockmuehl, "Bible Versus Theology: Is 'Theological Interpretation' the Answer?," *Nova et Vetera* 9, no. 1 (2011): 27-47.

[8]In another book I proposed this three-model approach with other terms: reading for retrieval, reading through the tradition, and reading with the tradition. See Scot McKnight, *The Blue Parakeet: Rethinking How You Read the Bible*, rev. ed. (Grand Rapids, MI: Zondervan, 2016), 25-36.

[9]Veeneman, *Introducing Theological Method*.

MODELS, IMPULSES, AND INTEGRATION

The two models may be briefly stated this way: the retrieval model believes everything done in systematics or constructive theology must be rooted in explicit biblical exegesis and texts, while the expansive model believes systematics begins with the Bible but over time has expanded considerably as our knowledge of God and truth and theology has progressed. The first wants to go back, and the second wants to explore for more. The first speaks more often about biblical theology and the second more often in terms of creedal, dogmatic, confessional, and systematic categories.[10]

Each model has to tangle with five separable but integrated and interrelated dimensions of theological truth claims:

1. the Bible

2. the creed

3. denominational confessions and doctrinal statements

4. major theologians forming a systematic theology

5. the multitude of theological explorations constantly at work in the history of the church in very specific locations and times

So, we have the (1) Bible and (2) the Niceno-Constantinopolitan Creed, with (for one example) (3) the Augsburg Confession, with (4) Karl Barth's *Church Dogmatics*, and with (5) Miroslav Volf's wonderful *Exclusion and Embrace* or (to give a second example of this fifth type) some decision made by the Anglican Church of North America to form its own catechism and Book of Common Prayer (both of which were shaped by specific theologians carrying weight).[11] Theology always has and always will be entangled in this web of five dimensions.

Now to describe the models.

---

[10]For a sketch of representative evangelical theologies, Veeneman, *Introducing Theological Method*, 81-110.

[11]Miroslav Volf, *Exclusion and Embrace: A Theological Exploration of Identity, Otherness, and Reconciliation*, rev. ed. (Nashville: Abingdon, 2019).

The retrieval model. The retrieval model's *impulse* is back to the Bible. *Sola Scriptura* here might not mean only the Bible, but it will certainly mean *prima Scriptura*, first the Bible.[12] All creeds, every denominational confession or statement of faith, all theologians, and every exploration that makes theological truth claims—it is argued in this model—have to justify their claims by appeal to the Bible. Even more: *appeal* here can mean "must be something the Bible is actually teaching" rather than something that can be hooked to a verse (however loosely).[13]

The retrieval model contends that *the fundamental form of theology is commentary on Scripture and the exposition of Scripture in preaching.* If God has chosen to speak to us in Scripture, then the Bible becomes

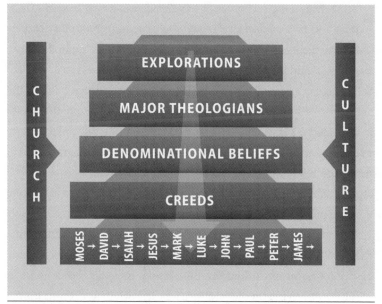

Figure 1.1. The retrieval model

[12]N. Clayton Croy, *Prima Scriptura: An Introduction to New Testament Interpretation* (Grand Rapids, MI: Baker Academic, 2011).

[13]The movement most tied to this approach is the Stone-Campbell movement or the Restoration churches: Churches of Christ and the Christian Church. For a good history, see Richard T. Hughes, *Reviving the Ancient Faith: The Story of Churches of Christ in America,* 2nd ed. (Abilene, TX: Abilene Christian University Press, 2008).

the sure foundation for all redemptive truths. Once one admits this or something close to it, theology becomes exegesis, commentary, and exposition of Scripture in light of the fullness of the Bible's gospel. One of the fundamental forms of doing theology, then, becomes preaching and teaching the people of God from Scripture. Which means that the retrieval model doesn't see whether the theologian has a few references to Scripture scattered here and there but looks for exegesis that is both aware of scholarship and oriented toward theological questions once it has probed the text in its own integrity. Some theologians claim this but don't do their theology this way. Some theologians claim their theology is Bible-only but are denomination-alists and read everything through their denominational theology.

The retrieval model contends that *theology is always in need of reformation* and *that biblical studies are also in need of constant reworking.* This is the Protestant principle of *semper reformanda* applied to both theological and biblical studies. Hence, the need always to go back to the sources (*ad fontes*). What drives this impulse to go back to the sources to rethink what we think is the confronting reality that God's truth is always bigger and better and greater than we can grasp. No one ever got it absolutely right. Everything in theology is a grasping but never the final grip. Hence, the retrieval model knows that biblical studies subvert by nature: they subvert what we think by confronting what we think with the gospel. The Bible, like Melchizedek, still speaks.

The retrieval model operates with *movement within the Bible* so that the New Testament's revelation of God in Christ has paradigmatic clarity for comprehending the Bible's own message. For some this will be a covenant-theology approach, for others a dispensational approach, while for others a redemptive-movement (or incremental) approach.[14] That is, God reveals the truth in a developmental way

---

[14]Geerhardus Vos, *Biblical Theology: Old and New Testaments* (Grand Rapids, MI: Eerdmans, 1948); Craig Alan Blaising and Darrell L. Bock, *Expansive Dispensationalism* (Grand Rapids, MI: Baker, 2000); William J. Webb, *Slaves, Women and Homosexuals: Exploring the Hermeneutics of Cultural Analysis* (Downers Grove, IL: InterVarsity Press, 2001).

from the days of Moses to Jesus through the apostles. In the broadest sense, we can call this a narrative approach to the Bible.

The retrieval model *knows the diversity of the Bible's own time-bound expressions.* What Moses said is not what David said is not what Isaiah said is not what Jesus said is not what Mark said is not what Luke said is not what John said is not what Paul said is not what Peter said is not what James said. Yet, what each later author says is somehow connected to what the predecessors said, and for many what the later authors say coheres with what the predecessors said. Furthermore, each brings to expression the truth of God in a given location for a given audience and expresses the thoughts of a given author. Many in the retrieval model dwell in peace with the Bible's own diversity and can preach Isaiah in his terms and then preach Hebrews in Hebrews' terms and not worry much about blending them into a systematic form. Such an approach forms Christian Bible readers into those who can appreciate diverse voices talking about great topics. At the same time, others will prefer one voice (Jesus, Paul, and John are the major voices that become dominant) over the others and either ignore the others or coerce the others into the shape of their preferred voice. I see this especially today with how people use the theology of Jesus or Paul.

There is something vital here that we biblical folks want to emphasize: the diversity of biblical authors, shaped as they are by context, requires that a single-minded approach to systematics often blunts the diversity of the Bible, and this silences alternative voices in the Bible itself. Very few theologians I read do well at combining or even articulating the kingdom vision of Jesus with the soteriological and ecclesiological vision of the apostle Paul, and that must butt up against the nearly complete absence of anything like a theology of Hebrews at work in systematic theologies. I'm not talking here about citing a verse from Hebrews here and there, especially when it comes to soteriology. No, I'm talking about the cosmic, spiritual, priestly vision of Hebrews that *frames that author's entire theology.*

The retrieval model *admits the ecclesial impact on the entire process.* On the left side of figure 1.1 above is "church," and this calls our attention to church influence on the whole process, and what this means is that reading the Bible itself is a church reading of Scripture. That church-shaped reading then shapes the entire history of theology itself. Some in the *sola Scriptura* approach actually believe and express that the Bible and the Bible alone is their creed, but such approaches are fanciful, however noble the focus on the Bible is. What is more, a highly individualistic approach to the Bible is against both how the Bible came to fruition (in the context of communities of faith in Israel and then in the church) and against how the Bible's formative teachings were formed (classical creedal orthodoxy). To go at it as if it were just "me and God" counters the very texts themselves.

The retrieval model *wants to check all developments and expansive understandings of gospel truth* with what the Bible says. What Athanasius, what Augustine, what Luther, what Calvin, what Wesley, what Edwards, what Hodge, what Schmemann, what Barth, what Rutledge, what Sonderegger, what Blount, what . . . whatever anyone said is valuable and meaningful, but the question the retrieval model presses on each of these noble theologians is, Is this a biblical idea or not? If it is not biblical, it will not necessarily be discarded, but it will be challenged to establish itself. Robert Jenson once said, "The question is not whether the church has this canon but whether this canon acknowledges the church."[15] Let me rework that: the question is not whether a theological system acknowledges Scripture but whether Scripture acknowledges that theological system.

The retrieval model (usually) *recognizes the impact of culture on every truth claim, every articulation, and every theology.* From Moses to the apostles, every Bible author and figure brought to expression truth claims about God that were shaped by and for a context. I have

---

[15]Robert W. Jenson, *Systematic Theology* (New York: Oxford University Press, 1997), 1:30.

called these "wiki-stories" of God's true story, but each wiki-story is but one approach to the one true story, and no wiki-story tells the whole story.[16] The same is to be said for the creeds, for denominational articulations, for the theologies of major theologians, and for the myriad of theological explorations. Each is connected to a context and has a specific location, with a specific author finding ways to explore truth claims about God. The recognition of cultural impact requires the biblical specialist to put each line and passage and author of Scripture in its historical context, and this is why there are so many Jewish and Greco-Roman contextual studies in biblical studies. The fruition of contextual studies in the twentieth and twenty-first centuries may well be the most important contribution made by those in biblical studies.[17] The oft-maligned but unavoidable and necessary historical-critical method, then, is hereby justified with full rigor.[18] The Spirit speaks then and to us because it is the same Spirit and the same people (the church).

The retrieval model *believes growth, development, and progress in theology only occur in preserving the Bible's truth claims and organically connecting all development to the Bible's original witness.* This is what it means to be in the retrieval model: it means *conserving* what is best in the past. In the history of the church, in fact in intellectual history itself, thinkers have composed what came to be called commonplace books, which recorded routinely the best insights and expressions and statements of what one was reading. One merely has to dip into something like Ann Moss's *Printed Commonplace-Books* or the I Tatti Renaissance Library volumes from Harvard University Press, or read someone who has made use of commonplace books today, such as

---

[16]McKnight, *Blue Parakeet.*

[17]For three quick examples, see Peter Lampe, *From Paul to Valentinus: Christians at Rome in the First Two Centuries,* ed. Marshall D. Johnson, trans. Michael Steinhauser (Minneapolis: Fortress, 2003); John H. Walton, *Genesis 1 as Ancient Cosmology* (Winona Lake, IN: Eisenbrauns, 2011); E. P. Sanders, *Judaism: Practice and Belief, 63 BCE–66 CE* (Minneapolis: Fortress, 2016).

[18]Jenson, *Systematic Theology,* 2:278-79.

Alan Jacobs, to see how these thinkers have done their best to conserve the best of those considered the best thinkers.[19]

To be conservative, then, is not to resist change. Rather, the very
term *conservative* is a theory of change. Not change for change's sake
but change *on the basis of organic connection to the best of the past*.[20] To
be in the retrieval model is to be intentionally unoriginal and non-
creative because one is a *tradent*. Put in biblical language, this is what
the Bible means by "wisdom." Yet, the retrieval model puts noticeable
constraints on theological exploration by requiring the exploration
to justify itself in the Bible's own truth claims. No matter how radical
some of his theological claims may be, Douglas Campbell's articulation of the apocalyptic approach to epistemology is a retrieval
mindset. All truth is to be measured by one criteria: the revelation of
the triune God in Christ (as articulated by Paul).

The dominant themes, then, are (1) back to the Bible, (2) measure
all truth claims by the Bible, and (3) let the Bible's own language
determine the shape of theology. Those most committed to this approach get under the skin the most with the next model.

The expansive model. Flip the retrieval model upside down and
one finds the expansive model, where the theological constructions
appear to be precariously perched atop the Bible and where one might
ask whether the Bible can hold it all up. Get too heavy on either side
and the whole thing tips and topples. Yet this is the reality of theological constructions. Theology always has and always will expand
the Bible's own truth claims and not just expound the Bible. Every
explanation *of* the Bible *expands or extends* the Bible.

The expansive model *begins with the Bible but expands what the Bible
says*. Every Sunday in my Anglican church (Church of the Redeemer

---

[19]Ann Moss, *Printed Commonplace-Books and the Structuring of Renaissance Thought* (New
York: Clarendon, 1996); Alan Jacobs, *Looking Before and After: Testimony and the Christian
Life*, Stob Lectures (Grand Rapids, MI: Eerdmans, 2008).

[20]This point draws on the theory of conservativism developed by Roger Scruton. See Scruton,
The Meaning of Conservatism, 3rd ed. (South Bend, IN: St. Augustine's Press, 2014); Scruton, *How to Be a Conservative* (London: Continuum, 2014).

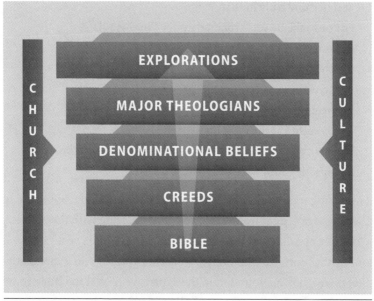

Figure 1.2. The expansive model

in Highwood, Illinois) we confess the Nicene Creed aloud. While the core gospel of 1 Corinthians 15 is at the base of the Nicene Creed (he suffered, was buried, rose again, will come again), what is said goes well beyond the simpler gospel affirmation of the apostles in 1 Corinthians 15. Here are Nicene's affirmations about the Son of God:

> We believe in one Lord, Jesus Christ,
> the only Son of God,
> eternally begotten of the Father,
> God from God, light from light,
> true God from true God,
> begotten, not made,
> of one Being with the Father;
> through him all things were made.
> For us and for our salvation
> he came down from heaven,
> was incarnate of the Holy Spirit and the Virgin Mary

and became truly human.
For our sake he was crucified under Pontius Pilate;
he suffered death and was buried.
On the third day he rose again
in accordance with the Scriptures;
he ascended into heaven
and is seated at the right hand of the Father.
He will come again in glory to judge the living and the dead,
and his kingdom will have no end.

I'm willing to say this is fully supportable in the Bible, but some of the language ("light from light" and "of one Being with the Father") comes from a different time, a different context, and speaks into and out of that context. Theology by nature explores and expands the Bible's own affirmations, but in the expansive model the Bible is the starting point. In some theological explorations the conclusions go well beyond the Bible, too far beyond the Bible, and at other times theologians will seemingly *assume* the Bible but barely tip their hat in its direction. As a Bible guy, I see this more vividly and surely more often than systematic theologians, but it must be emphasized that the Bible is the starting point for all Christian theology. There is a burgeoning development among traditional Christians today not only to embrace the classic creed but to embrace the worldview operative at the time.[21]

The expansive model's *impulse is to explore new dimensions of thinking as it carries forward the Christian biblical and theological tradition.*

---

[21]D. H. Williams, *Evangelicals and Tradition: The Formative Influence of the Early Church* (Grand Rapids, MI: Baker Academic, 2005); Hans Boersma, *Violence, Hospitality, and the Cross: Reappropriating the Atonement Tradition* (Grand Rapids, MI: Baker Academic, 2004); Boersma, *Sacramental Preaching: Sermons on the Hidden Presence of Christ* (Grand Rapids, MI: Baker Academic, 2016); Boersma, *Scripture as Real Presence: Sacramental Exegesis in the Early Church* (Grand Rapids, MI: Baker Academic, 2017); Gavin Ortlund, *Theological Retrieval for Evangelicals: Why We Need Our Past to Have a Future* (Wheaton, IL: Crossway, 2019). On the embrace of the classic creed today see the excellent book by Carl R. Trueman, *The Creedal Imperative* (Wheaton, IL: Crossway, 2012).

Growth, then, is the impulse. Progress, in other words. The trinitarian controversies of the third and fourth centuries, which have been (more than) fully explained by Lewis Ayres, are attempts to root theology in the Bible while seeking to explain the relationship of the Father, the Son, and the Spirit to one another in a way that preserves *oneness* while also clarifying *threeness*.[22] The soteriology of the church has paradigmatic terms and structures found in the sacrificial systems of the tabernacle and temple, but it was Paul's own articulations, especially in Romans, with terms such as *justification, redemption, reconciliation*, and *atonement*, that gave rise to the Reformation's clarifications that gave rise to various models of atonement in church theology. But let us not suppose that double imputation or Anselmian satisfaction theory or the various forms of substitutionary atonement theories are explicitly taught in the Bible just as we believe them today.[23] What many today consider the best atonement theory is often derivative from the atonement model at work in the gospel preaching that they initially affirmed.[24]

The expansive model *faces the constant temptation that is often called the "heresy of paraphrase," or the assumption or practice that theology's new formulations replace or improve on what the Bible says.* This is where those on the Bible side of this conversation dig in their heels. Yes, theology expands and extends because it seems to clarify and to systematize what the Bible says. But at times we Bible folks think the theologians have put the Bible in their rearview mirror and have moved on. So, a theology seems to be more rooted in the Luther or Calvin or Wesley or Edwards or Barth or Coakley than in the Bible itself.[25]

---

[22]Lewis Ayres, *Nicaea and Its Legacy: An Approach to Fourth-Century Theology* (New York: Oxford University Press, 2004).

[23]Boersma, *Violence, Hospitality, and the Cross*; Scot McKnight, *A Community Called Atonement* (Nashville: Abingdon, 2007).

[24]For instance, the scapegoat theory of the atonement found in René Girard, *I See Satan Fall Like Lightning*, trans. James G. Williams (Maryknoll, NY: Orbis, 2001).

[25]For "heresy of paraphrase," see John Webster, *The Culture of Theology*, ed. Ivor J. Davidson and Alden C. McCray (Grand Rapids, MI: Baker Academic, 2019), 77.

The expansive model *operates with the thoroughly biblical notion that the Spirit brings fresh light to the people of God in each generation.* One can claim the Spirit for whatever one wants, but the truth remains: the Spirit who was at work in Israel, in Jesus, in the early church, and in Scripture is the same Spirit at work in church of the past and in the church today. The leading verse that anchors this very notion in the Bible itself is from John 16:13: "When the Spirit of truth comes, he will guide you into all the truth; for he will not speak on his own, but will speak whatever he hears, and he will declare to you the things that are to come." The Spirit, Jesus told his own, "will guide you into all truth." To be sure, some claim falsehoods for truth, but silly claims does not the Spirit erase. Every theological context in every period of the church in every location of the church both needs and avails itself of the Spirit's guidance. Examples include the development of theology, the abolition of slavery, and rights for women.[26] One surely must think that theological growth has some anchor in the Spirit's own guidance.[27]

The expansive model *believes the Bible's own diversity and narratival development is the paradigm for ever-anew theological articulations.* The tendency of the retrieval model has been theological uniformity down to the precise terms, while there is an opportunity for the expansive model to make the Bible's own diverse theologies into a paradigm for theological diversity in the church. So the expansive model regrets the exclusion of diverse voices in the history of theology and intentionally invites diverse voices to the discussion, not so it can pat itself on the back and say, "What a woke thinker I am," but in order to listen and to learn and to change and to reform theology itself.

The expansive model, while it affirms the Bible's own formative framing of theological truth claims, *knows that each generation's articulations are context- and church-shaped for a specific time and place*

---

[26]I. Howard Marshall, with contributions from Kevin J. Vanhoozer and Stanley E. Porter, *Beyond the Bible: Moving from Scripture to Theology* (Grand Rapids, MI: Baker Academic, 2004).

[27]Kevin J. Vanhoozer and Daniel J. Treier, *Theology and the Mirror of Scripture: A Mere Evangelical Account* (Downers Grove, IL: IVP Academic, 2015), 116.

and people. Think about the Reformation (as Protestants see it). What happened? In one reading, Martin Luther, and later John Calvin, and later the (oft-ignored) Anabaptists, resisted the systemic imposition of Rome's power and theology and rediscovered the magnificence of the *by-grace-alone* potency of justification *by faith alone* all rooted in *sola Scriptura.*[28] There is not a Protestant theologian or pastor or church, and here I'm taking a bird's-eye view of what *Protestant* means, that doesn't operate on the basis of these ideas. Yet, each of those was formed in a context for a context, and that context shaped each of those ideas. Theology expands over time, but that growth often finds its climactic moments in specific contexts where something simply must be discerned. Sometimes that timely discernment becomes timeless, but other times it becomes time-bound.

The expansive model *builds organically on, but also disruptively with, the systematic visions of previous centuries.* What was said by Calvin for Calvin's day is not what needs to be said for our day in our way. In my life I can name some of the major theologians who have articulated for our time a message that speaks to our time—and here I span both biblical and systematic theology, and there is no attempt even to get close to representation: Karl Barth and Dietrich Bonhoeffer, Sarah Anne Coakley and Beth Felker Jones, Brian Blount and Eboni Marshall Turman, Soong Chan Rah and Grace Si-Jun Kim, N. T. Wright and Richard Hays, Beverly Gaventa and Fleming Rutledge. Each of these voices demonstrates organic connections to the church's theological tradition while also disrupting it and adding fresh ideas and challenging the old with critical clarities. What too often comes off as a Eurocentric discipline is actually a global reality.

The expansive model *assumes the truth that one can never return to the Bible-only world because knowledge, even knowledge of the Bible, is cumulative and developmental.* One cannot be a responsible theologian

---

[28]Kevin J. Vanhoozer, *Biblical Authority After Babel: Retrieving the Solas in the Spirit of Mere Protestant Christianity* (Grand Rapids, MI: Brazos, 2016).

and get behind Augustine, or behind Luther and Calvin, or behind Barth and Gutiérrez, or behind Mary Daly or Rosemary Radford Ruether. In biblical studies, which forms the basis for all theological reflections in the church, one can't get behind seminal studies by the likes of E. P. Sanders or Jewish scholars such as Jacob Neusner and Shaye Cohen. These seminal thinkers, as well as the creed and the theological affirmations of church bodies, have formed paradigms apart from which we do not think. Try as we might, it's impossible. Even those who have never read Augustine or Luther or Edwards will be shaped over time by their contributions, and many may well be thinking all they're doing is reading the Bible. They're not. They're reading a mediated Bible. Hence what is sometimes called a movement, the theological interpretation of Scripture.[29] Once we admit that our theologies are mediations of the Bible, we land somehow in an expansive camp.

These are the two major impulses for doing theology: retrieving the past or expanding our past into the present and future.

An integrative model. So, where are we? Enough has been said, I hope, for us to realize the retrieval model and the expansive model are both needed and are in fact both always at play in theological explorations. As a Bible specialist, however, I want to argue there is something not only *formative* about the Bible but also *authoritative*. Christians make the claim that the Bible is unlike all other books.

A model for doing Christian theology begins with the Bible, and we can call this *prima Scriptura*. But doing theology necessarily expands what the Bible says. Nonexpansive theology is limited to doing one thing: reading the Bible and repeating as closely as possible what it says. Within the pages of the Bible is a narrative that not only clarifies the plot from creation to kingdom but also expands, modifies, and re-expresses what has been said in the pages before it. Hence, the Bible itself provides a paradigm that can be reasonably called an expansive model.

---

[29]The movement now referred to as the "theological interpretation of Scripture" has been for me both a keen interest and a frustrating movement to define. I'm simply unsure what it means for me, a Bible interpreter.

Progress and expansion in theology, however, needs to be organically connected to the Bible's central theological truth claims. Hence, the back-to-the-Bible impulse of the retrieval model is as justified as the expansive impulse of the expansive model. They do not cancel each other out, but rather they form a dialectical relationship with each other, while the anchor is only tied to the Bible. Wisdom dictates that profound respect is to be given to the creed and to our own confessions and even to the theologians who light up our world, but the anchor is tied only to Scripture itself. Back and forth we go. So, one can call it the integrative model, and I hope to clarify this model in the chapters that follow. Markus Bockmuehl offers a firm reminder: "The Church receives and recognizes and teaches the canon of Holy Scripture; but the Church in both its unity and its diversity is constituted by and in response to the Word of God—rather than the other way round."[30]

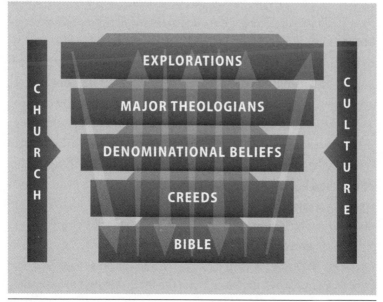

Figure 1.3. The integrative model

[30]Bockmuehl, "Bible Versus Theology," 35.

In this integrative model is the *ongoing dialectical back-and-forth* from Bible to modern theological articulations that are then challenged by the Bible as Bible people seek to constrain theological developments by what is in the Bible, while theologians continue to unfold the Bible and take it into fresh areas of thinking. All that is said above, then, could be restated here but need not be.

The integrative model, too, knows another dialectic. Namely, that the God who speaks in the Bible is the Trinity who speaks through humans. We *have* the Bible because God speaks, but we also only have the Bible because God's Spirit guided the church to recognize the Father's face in Christ in these Scriptures. But the Bible through which God speaks was written by human authors. We may well make the strong claim that 1–2 Chronicles is inspired by God, but there can be no gainsaying that the Chronicler was a fully individuated thinker who, facing the rebuilding of the temple at the time, told the story of Judah through the grid of temple worship. Hence, any devaluation of the human author by appealing to the divine author doesn't fit the Scriptures we have and know. One comes to know James in his frustration with what appears to be misreading of Paul just as one comes to know John with his particular vocabulary and syntax. To read the Bible from only one of these poles, then, is to misread the Bible and to set the course of theology on a slippery path. It is at the core of Christian conviction and theology that God comes first, and that both Israel and the church are effected by God as his creations, and it knows then that God is not a construction of the church. God does not, then, speak to Israel so much as God's speaking creates Israel, and the same pertains to the church. But God chose to give to Israel and to the church a voice in the Voice.[31]

The integrative model, if it operates with self-conscious integrity, *knows the Bible dimension of theology is foundational and not (as) final (as it might like to be).* Beginning with the Bible does not mean ending

---

[31]Thus, at times overstating one pole is Webster, *Culture of Theology*, 70-72, 119-23. Marcus Borg overstates the other: see Borg, *Reading the Bible Again for the First Time: Taking the Bible Seriously but Not Literally*, rev. ed. (San Francisco: HarperSanFrancisco, 2002).

with the Bible, though for the biblicists (see below) it often does. The integrative model begins in the Bible with exegetical finesse but recognizes that theology will start there but will develop in new directions because of new ideas, differing contexts, and diverse histories.

Now for a controversial point: the integrative model knows that *the Bible is fertile* and does not have to be restricted solely to authorial intent. As the prophets read their predecessors, as Jesus read the prophets, as Paul and the author of Hebrews and Peter and John read their Bible, they saw things not previously seen because Scripture is living and breathing and pulsating with throbbing possibilities. No one has spoken to this more provocatively or eloquently than David Steinmetz, who at the end of his essay "The Superiority of Pre-critical Exegesis," says,

> The defenders of the single-meaning theory usually concede that the medieval approach to the Bible met the religious needs of the Christian community, but that it did so at the unacceptable price of doing violence to the biblical text. The fact that the historical-critical method after two hundred years is still struggling for more than a precarious foothold in that same religious community is generally blamed on the ignorance and conservatism of the Christian laity and the sloth or moral cowardice of its pastors.
>
> I should like to suggest an alternative hypothesis. The medieval theory of levels of meaning in the biblical text, with all its undoubted defects, flourished because it is true, while the modern theory of a single meaning, with all its demonstrable virtues, struggles because it is false. Until the historical-critical method becomes critical of its own theoretical foundations and develops a hermeneutical theory adequate to the nature of the text that it is interpreting, it will remain restricted, as it deserves to be, to the guild and the academy, where the question of truth can endlessly be deferred.[32]

---

[32]David Steinmetz, *Taking the Long View: Christian Theology in Historical Perspective* (New York: Oxford University Press, 2011), 14.

The point was driven home to me years ago in the writings of Michael Fishbane.[33] A close reading of the New Testament texts makes me think we need a theory of Scripture that recognizes that what is biblical is suggestive of fresh ways of reading it as it is historical. By all means, find the author's intention and move on, and don't be surprised if your mind is opened to something you have never seen before.

The integrative model, then, dwells in an ongoing, never-ending, but flourishing reading of Scripture.

PRIMA SCRIPTURA: ALL THEOLOGIZING MUST BEGIN WITH SCRIPTURE

Only about the Bible do we say this: "All scripture is *inspired by God* and is useful for teaching, for reproof, for correction, and for training in righteousness, so that everyone who belongs to God may be proficient, equipped for every good work" (2 Tim 3:16-17). We might debate what *inspired* means, but the term in Greek is *theopneustos*, which more woodenly is "God-spirited" or "God-breathed." Something like this is found too in 2 Peter 1:21, that "no prophecy ever came by human will, but men and women moved by the Holy Spirit spoke from God." What Christians have claimed, then, on the basis of statements such as these is that the Bible is a book generated by God through one of God's prophets for the people of God.

What we mean by authoritative is that the Bible is a one-of-a-kind book, one fashioned in cooperation between God at work in the people of God and the author so that what is produced is a message from God. It functioned as revelation from God for ancient Israel, for Jesus, for the apostles, and for the church in its own history. Yes, yes, yes—of course, it has to be read and interpreted and articulated, and those articulations are not Scripture itself. We turn back to John 16:13 again to say that while we may have to admit in humility that our articulations can be off, we must also claim that God is good enough

---

[33]Michael Fishbane, *Biblical Interpretation in Ancient Israel* (Oxford: Clarendon, 1985).

and the Spirit clear about what is essential for our salvation. Caveats respected, there is nothing like Scripture for theology. It isn't just the first word in a long progression of words but what Kevin Vanhoozer calls the "norming norm."[34] A word above all other words. Such a text, then, requires receptive reverence on the part of the righteous reader. The posture of a Word of God reader is not mastery but listening in love and listening to learn and listening for living. We trust, we listen, we live, we love, and because we love, we live, we listen, and we trust.[35]

At the heart of much discussion about Scripture are the terms *infallibility* and *inerrancy*, both at their heart good terms and yet both fraught with debates, exaggerations, and hermeneutical implications—not to ignore boundary marking. I prefer a solid biblical term over these two terms, the term *truth*. In Hebrew *truth* is mostly *emunah/emet*:

> Do not take the word of truth utterly out of my mouth,
>   for my hope is in your ordinances. . . .
> Your righteousness is an everlasting righteousness,
>   and your law is the truth. . . .
> The sum of your word is truth;
>   and every one of your righteous ordinances endures
>   forever. (Ps 119:43, 142, 160)

The sense of the terms at work here has to do with reliability, faithfulness, and truth. In the first it is the word that is defined by truth, in the second the law/Torah is the truth, and in the third we have a summary statement: the *rosh*, or "head," of God's word is truth.

Only of the Logos of God, the revelatory acts of God, do we make the claim for truth. This is why we say of Jesus that he is the "way, and the truth, and the life" (Jn 14:6). Once we have landed on this

---

[34]Kevin J. Vanhoozer, *The Drama of Doctrine: A Canonical-Linguistic Approach to Christian Theology* (Louisville, KY: Westminster John Knox, 2005).

[35]Jacobs, *Theology of Reading*. Over and over one finds the same reverence for Scripture in Katherine Sonderegger, *Systematic Theology: The Doctrine of God* (Minneapolis: Fortress, 2015), 1:xvi, 9, 13, 66-77.

observation, we have stepped on a firm spot: *prima Scriptura* asserts itself because the *Scriptura* is true. All theology, then, must begin with Scripture as revelation of God's truth. Isaiah can say of God, "I the LORD speak the truth" (Is 45:19), and even King Nebuchadnezzar can say of Israel's God, "for all his works are truth" (Dan 4:37). Luke opens his Gospel by assuring Theophilus that he wrote the Gospel "so that you may know the truth" (Lk 1:4). John knows no limits: Jesus, the Word of God, is "full of grace and truth" (Jn 1:14), and the law comes through Moses, but "grace and truth came through Jesus Christ" (Jn 1:17). This one who is truth can be known in truth, and that "truth will make you free" (Jn 8:32), and this comes to us through the Spirit (Jn 14:17; 15:26; 16:13). "Your word," Jesus says, "is truth" (Jn 17:17). Paul thinks his preaching is about "truth" (2 Cor 4:2; 12:6; 13:8; Gal 2:5, 14; 4:16; Eph 1:13; 4:21; Col 1:5; 2 Thess 2:13; 1 Tim 2:4, 7; 3:15; 4:13; 2 Tim 2:15, 25; 3:7; Titus 1:1). Paul is not alone, for James speaks of truth (Jas 1:18; 5:19), and so too do Peter (1 Pet 1:22; 2 Pet 1:12) and John (1 Jn 1:8; 3:19; 4:6; 2 Jn 2, 4; 3 Jn 3, 4, 8, 12).

Theology, then, as the pursuit of truth about God, knows that the truth of the gospel revealed in Christ is the source of truth. For this reason we affirm in theological method *prima Scriptura*, and also in practice. Some theologians claim *prima Scriptura*, but their practice of theology falls short. John Webster's *The Culture of Theology* is an example: his book is about method in a broad sense, and he affirms Scripture and that theology is to be commentary on Scripture, but as I read the book I found precious little interaction with—let alone anything like commentary on—Scripture. Maybe this is the bias of my discipline coming through, and if it is: there it is. That's what I experienced reading Webster. This is not what I experienced reading a wonderful book by Irish theologian Patrick Mitchel, who is as biblical as he is theological in his exemplary study of love.[36] As Beth

---

[36]Patrick Mitchel, *The Message of Love: The Only Thing That Counts* (London: Inter-Varsity Press, 2019).

Felker Jones, a theologian, puts it in ways that not all would, "Christian theology is a conversation about Scripture, about how to read and interpret it better, how to understand the Bible as a whole and imagine a way of life that is faithful to the God whose Word this is."[37] Notice that for Jones, theology is a conversation about Scripture. *Prima Scriptura*. Her book exhibits just that.

While theology is clearly progressive in an expansive sense, it is called to pursue truth, which requires one to anchor one's theology in Scripture's witness to the one true God revealed in the way, the truth, and the life. This approach to theology is not a form of proof-texting, but it seeks the sure foundation on which all creeds, confessions, doctrinal statements, and explorations are to be constructed. Yet, the conversation that begins with Scripture continues, which Jones also states: "Theology begins with God's revelatory word to us. It continues as we respond with words: words to God and to each other." The "best practitioners," she reminds us, "are always ready to be challenged and corrected by God's Word."[38] This back-and-forth, this up and down on our images, is precisely what good theology is. It is part of the integrative model.

THE CHARGE OF BIBLICISM

I have made the point that good theology needs a constant return to Scripture, but returning to Scripture can itself go too far or pretend that Bible-only is the true method, so for good reasons Bible-focused theologians are sometimes accused of biblicism. In discussing this term in what follows, I anticipate the topic of the next chapter—not only do we go to Scripture first, but we must also heed the wisdom of the systematic theologians too. Now to the charge. Words such as *biblicism* are shot through with innuendo and become pejorative, and

---

[37]Beth Felker Jones, *Practicing Christian Doctrine: An Introduction to Thinking and Living Theologically* (Grand Rapids, MI: Baker Academic, 2014), 2. See too Vanhoozer and Treier, *Theology and the Mirror*, 106.

[38]Jones, *Practicing Christian Doctrine*, 12, 17.

running close behind the accusation of biblicism is the rhetorically not-so-subtle "and no one wants to be guilty of that, do they?" Kissing it on both cheeks is the accusation of bibliolatry, which is even worse than biblicism. For the biblical specialist, the retorts are "systematician" or "dogmatician" or "unbiblical" or "prolegomena-ism."[39] Markus Bockmuehl suggests that there is a ten-to-one ratio of biblicists to a more liberalized theological approach.[40]

What is biblicism? There are two uses of this term as I read the discussions, and I want to distinguish the two.[41] Kevin Vanhoozer and Daniel Treier define biblicism as "the supreme authority of Scripture."[42] They are affirming a very well-known set of categories used by an expert on the meaning of evangelicalism, namely David Bebbington.[43] Bebbington has marked evangelicalism with four major themes: (1) biblicism, (2) crucicentrism, (3) conversionism, and (4) activism.[44] If by biblicism one means only the Bible's supreme authority or even something like *prima Scriptura*, then I'd say it's fine, and that's what Bebbington meant. But I'm not sure the use of *ism* permits such a meaning to be clear. His *isms* are "centricities" more than "isms." So, I want to turn to a second use of *biblicism*. In this book, biblicism intentionally brackets off the theological tradition and so could be called *nuda Scriptura*, or *sola Scriptura* in the sense of *solo*.

---

[39]One person's exhilarating prolegomena is another person's "let's get on it with it." E.g., Sarah Coakley, *God, Sexuality, and the Self: An Essay "On the Trinity"* (Cambridge: Cambridge University Press, 2013), 1-99.

[40]Bockmuehl, "Bible Versus Theology," 32.

[41]I add another: *biblicism* is a synonym for "biblical scholars." So throughout Sarah Emanuel, *Humor, Resistance, and Jewish Cultural Persistence in the Book of Revelation: Roasting Rome* (New York: Cambridge University Press, 2020), e.g., 75.

[42]Vanhoozer and Treier, *Theology and the Mirror*, 12. On 102 they affirm *sola Scriptura* but not *solo Scriptura*: the second term is called subevangelical (as they say of some forms of biblicism), but their *solo Scriptura* is what in this book will be called biblicism. We are, then, more on the same page.

[43]David W. Bebbington, *The Dominance of Evangelicalism: The Age of Spurgeon and Moody* (Downers Grove, IL: IVP Academic, 2005).

[44]I have long followed scholarship about evangelicalism, and Bebbington's definition is about as widely accepted as any, but I no longer find defining it capable of anything approaching a consensus, nor do I find the term *evangelical* of much use in American discourse.

That is, "the Bible and the Bible alone" or "no creed but the Bible." To return to Vanhoozer and Treier, then, when on the next page they say they "believe that an evangelical account of first theology must extend the pattern of authority even further, to include the interpretation of Scripture in the church"—then I believe they are no longer biblicists (as used in this book).[45]

The biblicist wants to focus on the Bible and the Bible alone. To do so the biblicist methodically and intentionally brackets off the categories of the theologian. A theologian friend, when I asked him what *biblicism* means, wrote: "Biblicism = a literalistic approach to biblical authority and interpretation that intentionally ignores the theology of the church and the ancient (cultural) context of the biblical text."[46] Another theologian provided me with a fuller definition:

> an approach that regards the Bible as the exclusive source for formulating Christian belief and practice with explicit rejection of the need for historical background, garnering wisdom from the wider tradition, recognizing the influence of one's cultural location, and attaining insights from out-group perspectives even as it unconsciously replaces historical background with revered historical figures, rehearses its own tradition, reifies certain cultural values, and reinforces the in-group boundaries.[47]

I now illustrate with a parable. In a crabapple tree next to my reading chair, a black-capped chickadee discovered a small birdhouse, sometimes called a wren house. After inspecting the house and tree up and down, the chickadee and his wife went to work building a nest inside the birdhouse. While I was not able to watch every minute of their building to observe all their supplies and resources, when they were all done with hatching and brooding over their young and

---

[45]Vanhoozer and Treier, *Theology and the Mirror*, 13.

[46]Geoff Holsclaw, personal communication, May 6, 2020.

[47]Mike Bird, personal communication, May 6, 2020. Several others affirmed definitions much like these.

helping them learn the ways of bird life, I did open the birdhouse later to see what they used: wool, hair, moss, feathers, and string-like fibers. The first year they did this, not long after they were done, a pesky, mean-spirited house wren came by, poked his nosy head into the nest, and proceeded to dismantle the whole nest—grabbing stuff, returning to the opening, and dropping the nest to the ground. Not long after that, the chickadee returned and pitched a fit. That evening several fellow chickadees came by, perched on a phone line, and proceeded to pitch a fit in concert. They were, I take it, warning the wren not to try that again. Back to the birdhouse. The next year the chickadees did the same thing, and the third year they used their previous nest and improved it—a little removal, a little addition, and before long they had babies in their home.

One season later and as I was drafting this section, a house wren flew into our crabapple tree. It flitted around looking at our little wren house, inspecting it from all directions. It poked its head in and out of the house, flew around to inspect the back, top, both sides, and bottom of the house, and then returned to the front again. Before long it entered and began a quick demolition of what was left in the birdhouse from the previous year. The wren dipped into the house and quickly emerged with a mouthful of soft materials only to deposit them on the ground. Over and over until the job was done. The wren wanted the house cleared and clean before it could feel comfortable enough to make a nest for its eggs.

That's biblicism: clear the house of all vestiges of previous (theological) nests so one can make one's own theological nest. Biblicists are wrens.

Biblicism as used in this book means the bracketing or rejection of the church's theological tradition to go back to the Bible all over again and to begin all over again. To be a biblicist is to be a theological anarchist.[48] It is to bracket off the theological tradition of the church.

---

[48]A good example of the anarchist impulse can be found in Alan Hirsch and Michael Frost, *The Shaping of Things to Come: Innovation and Mission for the Twenty-First-Century Church*, rev. ed. (Grand Rapids, MI: Baker Books, 2013).

It is theologically, epistemologically, and ecclesiologically naive, but it's real. Biblicism is intentional disregard of the church's historic interpretations-become-theology/dogma.

The charge of biblicism, then, has some viability. Some, perhaps many, biblical scholars don't care about theology, especially as shaped by the creeds and confessions. The siloing effect has full play with such folks, but there's an underbelly here that is disturbing. Many biblical specialists are islands unto themselves—they study the Bible for themselves, the only ones who agree with them extensively are (a handful of) their students, and they live unto themselves. The intensity of personal study and discovery has led in many cases to scholars with results that are personally their own and no one else's, and sometimes sheer brilliance. Such persons are frustrated in churches because they think pastors are ignorant and systematicians are outdated, and they are right in one sense: if such a scholar is the measurement of the final word, those pastors and systematicians aren't listening to them. And why should they? This is one of the effects of biblicism, or theological anarchism, and it's the absolutizing of individual study of the Bible. (It may sound like I have experienced this, because I have.) Their favorite Bible verse could be 1 John 2:27: "As for you, the anointing that you received from him abides in you, *and so you do not need anyone to teach you.* But as his anointing teaches you about all things, and is true and is not a lie, and just as it has taught you, abide in him." This is not what this verse is talking about, but it mirrors the practice of many biblicists.

Biblicism exposed. Recently sociologist Christian Smith, formerly at the University of North Carolina and now at Notre Dame, has argued rather forcefully that biblicism in this second, anarchist sense defeats itself. The Bible *alone* creates a problem Smith labels "pervasive interpretive pluralism."[49] I summarize his major ideas now.

---

[49]Christian Smith, *The Bible Made Impossible: Why Biblicism Is Not a Truly Evangelical Reading of Scripture* (Grand Rapids, MI: Brazos, 2011).

Biblicism blankets much of evangelicalism as well as charismatic and Pentecostal Christianity where the Bible's exclusive authority, infallibility, or inerrancy, its perspicuity, self-sufficiency, consistency, universality, and self-evident meaning—a loaded list of terms, to be sure—pervade how the Bible is preached, taught, read, understood, and indwelled. So how does Smith define biblicism? Carefully, as it turns out. Too carefully for some, too comprehensively for others. He marks out ten elements of biblicism, and I have shortened his own brief explanations to give the gist of each:[50]

1. Divine writing: the Bible is identical to God's own words.

2. Total representation: the Bible is what God wants us to know and all God wants us to know in communicating the divine will to us.

3. Complete coverage: everything relevant to the Christian life is in the Bible.

4. Democratic perspicuity: any reasonable humans can read the Bible in his or her language and correctly understand the plain meaning of the text.

5. Commonsense hermeneutic: the plain meaning is there, just read it.

6. Solo (not *sola*) Scripture: we can read the Bible without the aid of creeds or confessions or historical church traditions (or systematic theology!).

7. Internal harmony: all passages on a given theme mesh together.

8. Universal applicability: the Bible is universally valid for all Christians, wherever and whenever.

9. Inductive method: sit down, read it, and put it together.

10. Handbook model: the Bible is intended by God to be a handbook or textbook for the Christian life.

---

[50]Smith, *Bible Made Impossible*, 4-5.

Smith contends biblicists who operate with these categories are guilty of "pervasive interpretive pluralism." Some illustrations, a few of which are mine and not Smith's, of pluralistic interpretations of what the Bible says include the following, and all one needs to see is that well-meaning people for each of these views believe that view is what the Bible teaches:

- Church polity: Presbyterian, Episcopalian, Free Church, Baptist, Roman Catholic?

- Baptism: immersion, trine immersion, pouring, sprinkling? Adults or infants?

- War: just war, pacifism, nonviolence, crusader theory?

- Atonement theory: classical theory, recapitulation, penal substitution, just substitution, representation, *Christus victor*, satisfaction, scapegoat, moral influence, governmental theory?

Of course, of course, each person in each category for each of these topics makes their case for their own beliefs, sometimes well enough to compel a paradigm shift. But, but, but . . . any knowledge of how such things work admits that over time we shift and change, and what is compelling at one time, or to one group of people, is not compelling at another time or to other groups. Smith's argument seems persuasive. The Bible alone, or biblicism, doesn't yield sufficient consensus and has generated an interpretive pluralism.[51]

---

[51]Vanhoozer and Treier weigh in about Smith and call what he describes "naïve (subevangelical) biblicism" (*Theology and the Mirror*, 85). This is what Smith means by "1." immediately below in the text. I don't think Vanhoozer and Treier face the problem of pluralism sufficiently, as Smith himself doesn't deny large areas of agreement but the theory of hermeneutics at work in biblicists. Both of these authors are robust theologians and so don't feel the weight of the biblicist challenge. I'm willing to call it naive as well, but that just means there are buckets of naiveté poured on congregations weekly, which takes us back to Smith. Their solution is not far from Smith's: a theologically sophisticated theology that constrains and forms our Bible reading. The difference is that Smith is Catholic and not a theologian, and they are "mere" evangelicals who are trained in theology and exegesis—and are good at it. Nor do either of them attend churches that have biblicistic preachers.

How to escape? Sometimes the response is a more radical version of the expansive model, that is, with something like liberalism, but Smith contends liberalism is not the solution, for it swings the other way and diminishes the church's theological orthodoxy as well as the Bible's perspicuity as it seeks to reread the Bible through modernity's categories.[52] How might committed biblicists respond to this problem of pervasive interpretive pluralism? Smith sketches six possible answers, but I mention only four:

1. Blame pervasive interpretive pluralism on deficient Bible readers: the reason we don't agree is that some are flat-out wrong, and if we'd get better at interpretation we'd (all) come to more consensus.

2. In an Augustinian move, one could blame the noetically damaged reader. Humans are corrupted in the mind, and so because of the fall we have plurality.

3. Blame (in effect) God: either God only wants some to know the fullness (listen in on theology and at times this actually is said, even if indirectly, but often in this way: very few are willing to embrace the fullness of the gospel, etc.) or Satan has blinded humans from seeing the truth.

4. Blame the human unwillingness to embrace ambiguity. There is for this view an inclusive higher synthesis, and the plurality of that synthesis reflects the truth, and the truth is much fuller and higher than many comprehend.

Smith's solution, however, is a Christocentric or Christotelic reading of the Bible, with all things leading to Christ and everything else falling away into details. His view smacks of some kind of Barthian Catholicism and is not to everyone's liking. Others will prefer other theological orientations.

---

[52]Roger E. Olson, *The Journey of Modern Theology: From Reconstruction to Deconstruction* (Downers Grove, IL: IVP Academic, 2013).

Biblicism defended and defeated. The irony is that one of Smith's biggest critics, John Frame, operates with the same (a theological) hermeneutic.[53] Frame, in defending biblicism against Smith, isn't a biblicist because he's a Reformed theologian whose theological tradition renders much that is a problem in biblicism inadequate. He is operating out of a creed-and-confession approach to Scripture.[54] There are three major theological traditions in the church: Orthodoxy, Catholicism, and Protestantism. Each of these traditions operates with a theological tradition that fills the reader's eyes with clear sight into the texts of Scripture. Which is to say, readers in each of these traditions have eschewed the anarchist impulse of biblicism. No tradition is more complete or potent for its readers than the Reformed tradition, so when Frame defends biblicism or counters Smith's accusations of biblicism, he does so *only because he isn't a biblicist.* The trick in this discussion is that the term *biblicism* changes meanings when it gets into the hand of one in a strong theological tradition.[55]

Frame calls into question some of the ten factors of Smith's biblicism, but Frame seems to miss the larger impact: Smith is accumulating largely shared characteristics of what biblicists believe about the Bible. One should think not of Frame's nuanced theology as guilty of biblicism, but of Wayne Grudem's big book on politics.[56] Frame wants to argue that good evangelicals don't do such things, and he is mostly right making the claim—the problem, however, is that in populist evangelicalism what Smith describes is a living, breathing reality. Therefore, there's lots of bad theology, and that's what Smith's

---

[53]John M. Frame, "Is Biblicism Impossible? A Review Article," *Reformed Faith & Practice* (September 2016), https://journal.rts.edu/article/is-biblicism-impossible-a-review-article/.

[54]Again, see Trueman, *Creedal Imperative.*

[55]Kevin DeYoung is another example. See his criticisms of Smith in DeYoung, "Those Tricksy Biblicists," Gospel Coalition, September 1, 2011, www.thegospelcoalition.org/blogs/kevin-deyoung/those-tricksy-biblicists/.

[56]Wayne A. Grudem, *Politics—According to the Bible: A Comprehensive Resource for Understanding Modern Political Issues in Light of Scripture* (Grand Rapids, MI: Zondervan Academic, 2010).

talking about. A rephrasing here and an adjustment there by Frame of the characteristics don't erase a movement.

Then Frame interacts with Smith's discussion of pervasive interpretive pluralism, largely admitting the embarrassing diversity, and puts on the table what Smith ignores: the massive agreement in theology in the church. But Frame then states that this kind of diversity happens because of how God has chosen to guide the church, and at this point he can say what he says *only because this does not threaten the substantial teachings of the Reformed tradition in which Frame himself dwells*. Sure, let the evangelicals dispute about baptism, because in his tradition it is infant baptism. What Frame gives away to Smith he can give because he operates within a tradition that undermines and escapes biblicism. I could be wrong in this, but I don't see in John Frame's writings anything that looks to me like biblicism. He is a theologically grounded interpreter of Scripture, and that theological grounding forms a tradition that *defines itself outside biblicism*. Frame reads the Bible through the Westminster Confession, and what he sees in the Bible he sees in part because of that tradition. No matter how you shuffle the cards, that approach to Bible reading is not biblicism.

I stand here with John Webster: "Theology has its controlling center in exegesis of Holy Scripture; Holy Scripture is the Word of God; the Word of God summons us to faithful reading."[57] But faithful reading is one shaped by the theological wisdom of the church and is not anarchist, which leads to the theme of our next chapter.

---

[57]Webster, *Culture of Theology*, 65.

THEOLOGY NEEDS TO KNOW ITS IMPACT ON BIBLICAL STUDIES

BIBLICAL SCHOLARSHIP IN THE LATE twentieth and early twenty-first centuries became interdisciplinary. It is not uncommon to find scholars who focus on history, on archaeology, on geography, on sociology, on literary criticism, on aesthetics, on ancient art and images—and more. No one scholar comprehends it all, but it is not difficult to discover that most passages in the Bible are subjected to multidisciplinary approaches. Theologians are even more multi-disciplinary, and one of the best examples of this today is Sarah Coakley. She explores gender theory, feminist criticisms, classic theology, history, art, and even field studies in modern church life as they affect theology's major themes. Top all this off with her penchant for exploring theology—the Trinity especially—through prayer and contemplation, or what she calls asceticism. Her own expression for her method is *théologie totale*. Anything of value comes into play, but her starting point—divine desire and human longing for God, and being loved by the other, which themselves are not disconnected from erotic desires—leads her to raid the cabinets of many disciplines.[1]

So, multidisciplinary studies are in vogue, with one very noticeable exception. Bible scholars break out in rashes about systematic theology's infiltration into biblical studies, so to get Bible scholars even to consider working with the discipline of theology can be an uphill trek with flat soles on oiled surfaces. Bible scholars, which means those whose expertise is either Old Testament or New Testament, live in constant tension with systematic theologians. We also have a disciplinary method that instructs us to base everything we think on the texts of the Bible. Another element of our method is to describe what a given biblical text meant by that author (the author's intention) in that world at that time. What, then, did Jesus mean by *kingdom* in a Jewish world? We eschew thinking about kingdom the way Abraham Kuyper did and ask what *kingdom* would have meant for a Jew, a Galilean Jew at that, in the first century when Herod Antipas was in charge. We ask what Paul meant by *faith* or *church* with his Jewish background: Tarsus was a major intellectual town, he was educated in Jerusalem in the Pharisee tradition, he met Christ on the road to Damascus, he was given a mission to the Gentiles, he conducted most of his ministry in the Diaspora and knew that back home in Jerusalem some Jewish Christians were not happy about what he expected, or didn't expect, of his Gentile converts. Many of my friends in the

---

[1]Divine desire and human longing for God connect here ineluctably with Schleiermacher's feeling of dependence; on the important connections of the two, see Nicola Hoggard Creegan, "The Winnowing and Hallowing of Doctrine: Extending the Program of the Father of Modern Theology?," in *Sarah Coakley and the Future of Systematic Theology*, ed. Janice McRandal (Minneapolis: Fortress, 2016), 115-37.

There has been a scuffle among some worship leaders that the development of "Jesus is my boyfriend/lover" or "God is my lover" songs are unworthy of serious theology. One wonders whether such leaders have read Hosea or know the rich and developed history of how the Song of Solomon has been read in both Christianity and Judaism. Coakley has now ended the debate, without sanctioning shallow words. I recommend reading chapter six first, as it gives the categories and center of her entire argument. See Sarah Coakley, *God, Sexuality, and the Self: An Essay "On the Trinity"* (Cambridge: Cambridge University Press, 2013).

academic world of Bible scholarship see themselves as historians far more than as theologians.

So the questions that need to be asked of every Bible scholar run along these lines: Just how Christian is our description of our author-in-context? And do we expect everyone to believe what we think we have discovered? Do Bible scholars believe we should bracket off the creeds of the church, the statements of faith, and the confessions until we get our work done? When do we begin theology? Where do we begin it? Is description of the biblical text in context sufficient for doing theology?[2]

This chapter will conclude with one major finding: Bible scholars can't get to the church's faith without listening to the church's faith in their own Bible studies. Theologians, I am here to admit and confess, are needed by biblical scholars if they want to read the Bible well for the church. To show this, I want to walk us through some not-quite-there studies of Christology by some of the finest scholars of the New Testament in the twentieth and early twenty-first centuries, and then we will turn to some other scholars who have, instead, listened to the church and found dimensions of New Testament Christology that the others did not find. But first, a reminder of the church's faith.

LISTENING TO THE CREED

A brief reminder that this is what the church believes, and this is what (at least) some of us say aloud each Sunday when we gather for fellowship and worship and publicly confess:

> We believe in one Lord, Jesus Christ,
> the only Son of God,
> eternally begotten of the Father,
> God from God, light from light,

---

[2]See Dale B. Martin, *Pedagogy of the Bible: An Analysis and Proposal* (Louisville, KY: Westminster John Knox, 2008).

true God from true God,

begotten, not made,

of one Being with the Father;

through him all things were made.

For us and for our salvation

he came down from heaven,

was incarnate of the Holy Spirit and the Virgin Mary

and became truly human.

For our sake he was crucified under Pontius Pilate;

he suffered death and was buried.

On the third day he rose again

in accordance with the Scriptures;

he ascended into heaven

and is seated at the right hand of the Father.

He will come again in glory to judge the living and the dead,

and his kingdom will have no end.

Attached to the Nicene creed is the understanding of Christ at Chalcedon, well beyond the New Testament, and yet we ask—as we are in this chapter—whether these categories might help us comprehend what the apostles are actually getting at:

Therefore, following the holy fathers, we all with one accord teach men to acknowledge one and the same Son, our Lord Jesus Christ, at once complete in Godhead and complete in manhood, truly God and truly man, consisting also of a reasonable soul and body; of one substance (*homoousios*) with the Father as regards his Godhead, and at the same time of one substance with us as regards his manhood; like us in all respects, apart from sin; as regards his Godhead, begotten of the Father before the ages, but yet as regards his manhood begotten, for us men and for our salvation, of Mary the Virgin, the God-bearer (Theotokos); one and the same Christ, Son, Lord, Only-begotten, recognized in two natures, without confusion, without change, without division, without separation; the distinction of natures being in no way annulled by the union, but rather the characteristics of each nature being preserved and coming together to form one person and subsistence, not as parted or separated into two persons, but one and the same Son and Only-begotten God the Word, Lord Jesus Christ; even as the prophets from earliest times spoke of him, and our Lord Jesus Christ himself taught us, and the creed of the Fathers has handed down to us. (Council of Chalcedon, 451 AD, Act V, from the Book of Common Prayer)

It is a long and winding road from the New Testament to Chalcedon, but I wonder whether that distance might be shortened if we would but listen to the creedal formations in the church more carefully and let their thoughts give us new heuristics. Is it perhaps not honest of us to affirm what Robert Jenson says when he writes, "Historical honesty requires the church to interpret Scripture in the light of her dogmas"?[3] It's time for us to ponder that very question. (Another way of asking it is whether it is possible even to interpret Scripture apart from the church's dogmas. An easy yes here is not as easy as many might think.)

APPROACHES THAT NARROW THE VOICE

James D. G. Dunn. I was on my way to becoming a student of James D. G. Dunn when he sent me a copy of his brand-new and quite controversial book *Christology in the Making.*[4] Entering into a flashpoint theological topic at the time with John Hick, concerning whether Jesus was divine and whether New Testament authors believed in the preexistence of Jesus, Dunn examined major New Testament christological categories to see whether the authors affirmed

---

[3]Robert W. Jenson, *Systematic Theology* (New York: Oxford University Press, 1997), 2:281.
[4]James D. G. Dunn, *Christology in the Making: A New Testament Inquiry into the Origins of the Doctrine of the Incarnation*, 2nd ed. (Philadelphia: Westminster John Knox, 1989).

the incarnation as he probed the origins of incarnation theology. It would not be possible here to go through Dunn's work in a way that would be thorough and, fortunately, that is not needed for the task at hand. A snapshot is that these categories are on a crescendo from no to yes.

I offer a summary, then, of this major work, and it begins with the assumption that first-century Judaism was monotheistic to the core.[5] To be Jewish was to believe in one God, and to be a Christian Jew was to believe in one God. The tension was felt over how exalted Jesus could be perceived to be while maintaining monotheism. First, Dunn concluded that nothing in the Jewish or Greco-Roman world provided evidence for a belief that God or angels or gods or so-called intermediary figures would become human for the redemption of humans. Second, Jesus did not think of himself as God incarnate, though he did claim to have a special intimacy with God as a Son does to the Father, but incarnation, Dunn argues, is not something to be found in the earliest levels of the Gospels. Third, first-generation Christianity was reshaped by belief in the resurrection of Jesus, which led early Christians to comprehend Jesus in light of the Old Testament's major figures—such as Adam and Wisdom and the Son of Man in Daniel 7. Dunn argued that these various understandings of Jesus (Jesus as second Adam, Jesus as Wisdom, Jesus as Son of Man) were not evidence of preexistence or incarnation, but he did conclude that later New Testament texts (such as the Gospel of John) set the tone for later developments of trinitarian thinking. Thus, in John, Hebrews, and even Matthew we begin to see the doctrine of incarnation and preexistence. Dunn's conclusion was that the doctrine emerged late in first-century Christianity, but only in John is it full-blown.

Notice that Dunn offers a careful piece of history based on historical methods of determining dates and layers of early Christian

---

[5]The following is all based on the second edition, some of which was not in the first edition.

christological reflection that led him to see incarnation as only ap-
pearing in the latest levels of the New Testament. The New Testament,
obviously, does not teach Nicene Christology but something less (if
I may) and something more diverse. A trajectory can be found from
Jesus to John's Gospel, but it is but one of the trajectories that one
might choose to chase. When Dunn was criticized by traditionalists,
he appealed to two major ideas: his conviction that we are to pursue
the "historical context of meaning" and an admission of "conceptu-
ality in transition." Dunn's method was historical exegesis in the
historical-critical mode, and his conclusions challenge creedal Christians to rethink what the New Testament actually teaches as it develops. His conclusions, then, affirm an expansive model of theology.

Dunn, however, was not done with this discussion, as he continued
to articulate and nuance a progressive christological movement in the
context of adhering to Jewish monotheism.[6] Alongside these nuanced
articulations by Dunn, another New Testament specialist, Larry
Hurtado, disagreed sharply with Dunn by maintaining that very early
Jewish Christians were worshiping Jesus alongside God (the Father).
Debate between Dunn and Hurtado turned into a book by Dunn
called *Did the First Christians Worship Jesus?*[7] In this book Dunn warns
of "Jesus-olatry" as a near parallel to ancient prophetic warnings about
idolatry. Early Christian worship, he contends, was *in* Christ and
through Christ, but not so commonly was it a worship *of* Christ. True
Christian worship is the worship of the Father of our Lord Jesus Christ,
offered in the Spirit, through the revelation of that God in Christ.

Where do Dunn's conclusions lead us? To less than the creed, less
than the church's faith. Dunn, who passed away as this book was in

---

[6]James D. G. Dunn, *The Theology of Paul the Apostle* (Grand Rapids, MI: Eerdmans, 1998),
266-93; Dunn, *The Partings of the Ways: Between Christianity and Judaism and Their Significance for the Character of Christianity* (Philadelphia: Trinity Press International, 1991).
[7]James D. G. Dunn, *Did the First Christians Worship Jesus? The New Testament Evidence*
(Louisville, KY: Westminster John Knox, 2010).

process, was a Methodist who weekly affirmed the creed while knowing that what the creed states explicitly and what the church's theologians have affirmed for centuries as part of the expansive model's development of Christian theology. He does not deny that theology, but his method brackets off those categories and then concludes that they are not present in Scripture. Is this the way we are to do theology?

Larry Hurtado. Hurtado, who also recently passed away, has become perhaps the world's most significant early church "Christologian." From his 1988 *One Lord, One God* to his *Lord Jesus Christ* and then to the summary of all his work in a small volume, *Honoring the Son*, Hurtado maintains one distinct line of thinking: the earliest Christians worshiped Jesus alongside God.[8] His approach to the christological question—How divine is Jesus?—is through early Christian experience and devotion, and Hurtado has undoubtedly advanced the discussion and elevated Jesus above all his contemporaries, but like Dunn he falls short of classic Christian orthodoxy in not achieving a trinitarian theology.

Hurtado, in a number of locations and in different ordering, points to six features of early Christian worship that indicate Jesus was being worshiped alongside God/Father, and this for Hurtado fits into the mutation of monotheism that he often also calls "binitarian."[9] Briefly I summarize each of Hurtado's points. First, prayer was offered in Jesus' name and through him, something Hurtado is aware was not found elsewhere in the ancient world:

> First, I thank my God *through Jesus Christ* for all of you, because your faith is proclaimed throughout the world. (Rom 1:8)

---

[8]Larry W. Hurtado, *One God, One Lord*, 3rd ed. (New York: Bloomsbury T&T Clark, 2015); Hurtado, *At the Origins of Christian Worship: The Context and Character of Earliest Christian Devotion* (Grand Rapids, MI: Eerdmans, 1999); Hurtado, *Lord Jesus Christ: Devotion to Jesus in Earliest Christianity* (Grand Rapids, MI: Eerdmans, 2003); Hurtado, *How on Earth Did Jesus Become a God? Historical Questions About Earliest Devotion to Jesus* (Grand Rapids, MI: Eerdmans, 2005); Hurtado, *Ancient Jewish Monotheism and Early Christian Jesus-Devotion: The Context and Character of Christological Faith* (Waco, TX: Baylor University Press, 2017).
[9]Hurtado, *At the Origins*, 70-97. What follows comes from these pages.

On that day you will ask nothing of me. Very truly, I tell you, if you ask anything of the Father *in my name*, he will give it to you. Until now you have not asked for anything *in my name*. Ask and you will receive, so that your joy may be complete. (Jn 16:23-24)

Next, recognizing the constant early Christian use of *Lord* for Jesus and not for the Father, it appears Jesus could be addressed in prayer in a text such as 1 Thessalonians 3:11-13 ("Now may our God and Father *and the Lord Jesus* direct our way to you. And may *the Lord* make you increase . . . and may *he* so strengthen your hearts"), but for sure Jesus is directly addressed in prayer in 2 Corinthians 12:8-9: "Three times I appealed *to the Lord* about this, that it would leave me, but he said to me, 'My grace is sufficient for you, for power is made perfect in weakness.' So, I will boast all the more gladly of my weaknesses, so that the power of Christ may dwell in me." Add to this the prayer of Stephen in Acts 7:59-60 ("*Lord*, do not hold this sin against them") and we have prayer addressed to Jesus (see too Acts 13:2). Second, early Christian invocations and confessions were Christ-focused. A preeminent example, one studied in a number of contexts by Hurtado, is *maranatha* (1 Cor 16:22), which is an invocation for Christ the Lord (Aramaic *mar*) either to be present or to come back soon. Again, this was language used only for God among Jews and was now being used for Jesus in a gathering for worship. Alongside this Hurtado reminds us of the confession of Jesus as Lord in Romans 10:9-13, where the Old Testament language of "calling upon the name of the Lord" is appropriated for Jesus (see 1 Cor 12:3; Phil 2:11), and once again it is the liturgical, worship setting that sends shivers up the spine of most strict monotheists. As well, in 1 Corinthians 5:4 we read, "When you meet together *in the name of our Lord Jesus*" (CEB), and we encounter a worship gathering framed by the Lord Jesus.[10]

---

[10]Both the NRSV and NIV are not as clear here as the CEB.

For his third example of early Christian Christ-framed worship, Hurtado looks at baptism, and here we can simply observe that early baptism was "in the name of Jesus" (Acts 2:38; 8:16; 10:48). No baptismal practice in Judaism has such a ritual in the name of a person, and such a ritual wording indicates Jesus as the Agent of redemption (see also Gal 3:27; Rom 6:3). Such persons, Paul says, "have clothed yourselves with Christ" (Gal 3:27). This ritual act of baptism, diminished in so many churches today to the point that the remarkable nature of this wording slips by, plunges a person into the redemptive world created by Christ and puts the person in a position of devotion to Christ.

Fourth, Hurtado shows how the Lord's Supper in early Christian gatherings was focused on Christ. This meal, and Hurtado's emphasis deserves repetition in our world, was cultic and not just an ordinary, common meal. It was not an ordinary meal, for it was the "Lord's" Supper and the "cup of the Lord" (1 Cor 10:21; 11:20). Such a meal, then, was not simply an act of recall or even a subtle connection to the Lord but a celebratory meal of redemption. Hurtado puts this in the following terms: "In short, the cult-meal of the Christian congregation is here emphatically one in which the Lord Jesus plays a role that is explicitly likened to that of the deities of the pagan cults and of God! This is not merely a memorial feast for a dead hero. Jesus is portrayed at it, and with whom believers have fellowship as with a god."[11] As with the first three categories of Hurtado's, so also here: what was done by Christians in the Lord's Supper was unprecedented in Judaism.

What has struck most about the Christology of the early Christians is Hurtado's fifth category of early Christian devotion: hymns to Christ. The early followers of Jesus sang with one another (see Acts 16:25; 1 Cor 14:26; Eph 5:18-20; Col 3:16-17), but it was the discovery of early Christian songs or hymns embedded in the letters of

---

[11]Hurtado, *At the Origins*, 85.

Paul that takes the songs to the next level in Christology. We are talking here about Philippians 2:6-11 and Colossians 1:15-20, and Hurtado includes also John 1:1-18; Ephesians 5:14; and 1 Timothy 3:16.[12] These songs celebrate the work of Christ (the Son), not God (the Father) and, as songs, no doubt were adjoined to the public use of the Psalms. As Hurtado suggests, such use of the Psalms itself would have led early believers to see Christ in Israel's songbook. Hurtado then adduces hymns found elsewhere, such as Luke 1:46-55, 67-79; 2:29-32; and Revelation 5:9-11. Focusing on Christ in the assembly's hymns marked the Christians off from all other groups in the ancient world, and at the center was the exaltation of Christ. For all creation to bow to Jesus, as is seen in Philippians 2:6-11, borders on breaching the walls of monotheism. In Hurtado's terms, Jesus was worshiped alongside God. Hurtado's final category, early Christian prophecy, connects us once again to using common Old Testament expressions—the word of the Lord, as the Lord says—to now words attributed by Christian prophets to the Lord Jesus. He points us to Acts 9:10-17 as well as the well-known prophetic words to the seven churches of Revelation (Rev 2–3).[13]

Where does this take us? Beside the attractiveness of this display of careful scholarship and attentiveness to social realities, Hurtado's work gets us no further than binitarianism (Father, Son) and yet "an exclusivistic monotheism."[14] In this Hurtado pushes beyond Dunn but falls short of classic orthodoxy. One can ask whether bracketing out later trinitarian categories prevents the historian from seeing

---

[12]Matthew E. Gordley, *The Colossian Hymn in Context: An Exegesis in Light of Jewish and Greco-Roman Hymnic and Epistolary Conventions*, Wissenschaftliche Untersuchungen zum Neuen Testament 2/228 (Tübingen: Mohr Siebeck, 2007); Gordley, *Teaching Through Song in Antiquity: Didactic Hymnody Among Greeks, Romans, Jews, and Christians*, Wissenschaftliche Untersuchungen zum Neuen Testament 2/302 (Tübingen: Mohr Siebeck, 2011); Gordley, *New Testament Christological Hymns: Exploring Texts, Contexts, and Significance* (Downers Grove, IL: IVP Academic, 2018).

[13]He adds 1 Cor 14:37-38; 2 Cor 12:9; 1 Thess 4:2, 15-17; 2 Thess 3:6, 12.

[14]Hurtado, *At the Origins*, 95.

patterns of trinitarian thinking in the early church. Like Dunn, the exaltation of Christ for Hurtado is ultimately the act of assigning such a role to Christ. He is the God-appointed Lord, and this confession is a mutation of monotheism but relentlessly remaining monotheism. In his massive and summary statement in *Lord Jesus Christ*, Hurtado changes his former expression "mutation" to "a distinctive variant form of monotheism."[15]

Yet, Hurtado explicitly recognizes what he calls the "triadic" shape of God discourse in the New Testament, a discourse that reflects the experience of the earliest Christians.[16] A few observations about this development in Hurtado's thinking. It is impossible to talk about God in the New Testament and not talk about Jesus (and to a lesser degree about the Spirit), but it would be anachronistic to talk in language of the later classic creeds. Hurtado, however, says the early Christian language made later theological categories such as person and substance "unavoidable."[17] In his view the language of the New Testament tends to be monodirectional—the Father sends, the Son obeys, the Spirit is sent. The Son does not send, the Spirit does not send, and the Father does not obey and is not sent. Yet, I believe it was the early Christian discourse and the Christian experience of God—the Father, the Son, the Spirit—that gave rise to Trinity thinking, and without that first-century experience the later theological development would not have occurred. Like Dunn thinks, the New Testament is a point along the way to later trinitarian theology. There is, then, for Hurtado a three-ish-ness to early Christian God discourse, a three-ish-ness that has an emphatic binitarian as well as God-focused shape. As I have said, it falls short of classic orthodoxy.

It is not possible here to delve into all the contours of Hurtado's thinking, and he presses into monotheism as he presses against

---

[15]Hurtado, *Lord Jesus Christ*, 50. But he returns to "mutation" in Larry W. Hurtado, *God in New Testament Theology* (Nashville: Abingdon, 2010).

[16]Hurtado, *God in New Testament Theology*, 99-110. What follows comes from these pages.

[17]Hurtado, *God in New Testament Theology*, 100.

Dunn's view of monotheism, but I have given enough of his work to indicate the genius contribution to understanding early Christology as well as how it falls short of classic orthodoxy. Is this, I ask, how Christians are to do theology? Do we preach and teach early Christian binitarian thinking, or is there perhaps another way?

Richard Bauckham. Discussions of the deity of Christ or, perhaps more delicately, how divine Christ was in the theology of Jesus and the apostles, has been engaged from yet another angle by Richard Bauckham, who presses into service the category of divine identity and asks whether Jesus was perceived as part of that divine identity. Bauckham does so, as with Dunn and Hurtado, from the category of Jewish monotheism.[18] The work of Hurtado and the work of Bauckham overlap in substantive ways, and this permits me (in this context) to summarize Bauckham more quickly. Both examine elements that point in the direction of the deity of Christ, Hurtado toward elements connected to the experience of worship and Bauckham to claims about Jesus.

Bauckham outlines the following elements: (1) the use of Psalm 110:1 for Jesus ("The LORD says to my lord"; cf. Heb 1:13), (2) the sovereignty of Jesus over all (e.g., 1 Cor 15:27-28), (3) that Jesus shares God's exalted status beyond all the powers (Eph 1:21-22), (4) that Jesus is given the divine name (Phil 2:9), (5) the worship of Jesus in Revelation 5, and (6) that the preexistent Christ created (Jn 1:1-5; 1 Cor 8:6). For Bauckham, Judaism believed in one God (monotheism), and what distinguished that God was creating and ruling all of creation, and this unique identity of God led Jews to worship that one God. Worship—and here is another tie to Hurtado's work—of God is distinguished from Jewish beliefs about all intermediary figures. The Word and Wisdom of God do participate in both God's

---

[18]Richard Bauckham, *Jesus and the God of Israel: God Crucified and Other Studies on the New Testament's Christology of Divine Identity* (Grand Rapids, MI: Eerdmans, 2008). The summary here comes from this book, especially 18-59.

creation and God's ruling and so figure into the unique identity of
God. This sets the stage for early Christian beliefs about Jesus as Word
and Wisdom. To anticipate what will be said by Wesley Hill below,
Bauckham seeks to show that Jewish monotheism can permit Jesus
to participate in the unique divine identity, and so he speaks of a
"Christology of divine identity."[19]

Bauckham, however, goes further than Hurtado in spelling out *who
God is* on the basis of *the earthly Jesus*. That is, the one who lived and
died is the one who is part of the divine identity and reveals that
divine identity. Put as Bauckham does, "the christological pattern of
humiliation and exaltation is recognized as revelatory of God."[20]
Again, he sketches his view in a number of observations about the
early Christian use of Isaiah 40–55 and the Suffering Servant as paradigmatic for Christology. To counter other theologies, God is not
hidden but revealed *for who God is* in the cross, which is to say that
God reveals his deity in the crucifixion. He is God crucified.

Noteworthy in both Hurtado and Bauckham is that their own
perceptions of early Christology are that it was very early and much
earlier than permitted by Dunn, for whom a high Christology did not
form until the later layers of the New Testament, most especially with
John. Bauckham, however, claims that the development models of
Christology and trinitarian thinking are flawed. Rather, it's all there.
Classical orthodoxy is not Hellenistic ideas imposed on Jewish monotheism but, instead, as he frames it:

> The conceptual shift from Jewish to Greek categories was from
> categories focused on divine identity—who God is—to cate-
> gories focused on divine being or nature—what God is. The
> creedal slogan of Nicene theology—the *homoousion* (that Christ
> is of the same substance as the Father)—may look initially like
> a complete capitulation to Greek categories. But the impression

---

[19]Bauckham, *Jesus and the God*, 32.
[20]Bauckham, *Jesus and the God*, 33.

is different when we understand its function within the Trinitarian and narrative context it has in, for example, the Nicene and Niceno-Constantinopolitan Creeds. This context identifies God as Father, Son and Holy Spirit, and identifies God from the narrative of the history of Jesus. The *homoousion* in this context functions to ensure that this divine identity is truly the identity of the one and only God. In its own way it expresses the christological monotheism of the New Testament.[21]

Yet, Bauckham—a true biblical specialist who both knows and challenges systematicians—contends the classic creeds did not get the fullness of the early Christians' crucified God theology: "Adequate theological appropriation of the deepest insights of New Testament christology, such as we have observed in Philippians 2:6-11 and the Fourth Gospel, was not to occur until Martin Luther, Karl Barth and more recent theologies of the cross."[22]

Where then are we? At the summit of Mount Nebo, if you will. We can see the land, we can see the Jordan, but, like Moses, we will not cross the river to enter the land because we have fallen short. How so?

I turn first to a crucial contribution when it comes to mapping the relationship of biblical studies to theological studies, namely, to Wesley Hill's recent book *Paul and the Trinity: Person, Relations, and the Pauline Letters*. A brief word needs to be said that I am not suggesting, nor do I believe, that the three scholars discussed below are imposing the substance of the creed on New Testament texts. Rather, they are open to not bracketing off the later substance of Christian theology as they seek to explore what the New Testament says.

---

[21]Bauckham, *Jesus and the God*, 58-59.
[22]Bauckham, *Jesus and the God*, 59. Like Dunn and Hurtado, and as different from them as they are from each other, is N. T. Wright's creative theory that Jesus' entry to Jerusalem in the last week was the return of Israel's God, YHWH, to Zion. This is another example of christological monotheism that does not use later categories to probe the New Testament. See Wright, *Jesus and the Victory of God*, Christian Origins and the Question of God 2 (Minneapolis: Fortress, 1996), 612-53.

STUDIES THAT EXPAND THE VOICE

Wesley Hill. Because I have summarized already the Christologies of Dunn, Hurtado, and Bauckham, something Hill does more comprehensively in his book, this portion of the chapter can focus more on Hill's distinctive contribution, which I believe is paradigm shifting for the study of early Christian Christology. First, Hill categorizes the Dunn-to-Bauckham analyses as occurring on a vertical axis from low to high, with Dunn at the low end, Hurtado higher, and Bauckham higher yet. But a vertical axis is neither high enough nor adequate to how the apostle Paul (and one could speak here also of John and Hebrews) describes God and Christ. Hill contends that New Testament scholars, as historians, have rejected or simply ignored later Christian patterns of thinking that, while more precise in their later formulations, are nonetheless present in the early layers of New Testament Christology. The question being asked by the above described scholars is, How high can we go with Christ? Is he as high as God on the vertical axis or not?

Hill proposes another axis, one marked by persons and mutualities and relationships. Hill probably goes too far in posing his view *against* those views in that the issue of how high is already present in the New Testament when Jesus is accused of blasphemy or when someone asks, "Who does he think he is?" But Hill is certainly correct in contending that the vertical axis is insufficient *for describing what is already present in the New Testament itself.*

> Instead of starting with God and attempting to fit Jesus and the Spirit alongside or underneath him somewhere on an axis of nearness, it is better . . . to see neither God, Jesus, nor the Spirit as enjoying primacy on their own but to see them *all as equally primal, mutually determinative, relationally constituted.* "God," on this account, is unspecifiable apart from Jesus and the Spirit; likewise, "Jesus" is unknowable apart from his relations with

God and the Spirit; and "the Spirit" is impossible to identify without God and Jesus. *Together, all three exist in a web or skein of relationality that makes each of the three who they are.*[23]

Hill is not alone in proposing this, and he points to previous scholars such as Nils Dahl, Leander Keck, and C. Kavin Rowe. It is Hill through whom this has become for me a convincing illustration of the need for New Testament scholars to listen to the theologians of the church, namely, the creeds and those theologians behind the major creeds, and not bracket off later thinking as impossibly later categories.

What Hill does in his book—and the details can be found in a careful reading of *Paul and the Trinity*—is to demonstrate that God (Father) is conceptualized in relationship to the Son and the Spirit, and the Son in relation to the Father and Spirit, and the Spirit in relation to the Father and Son. Jewish monotheism, when made so paradigmatic for some scholars, *brackets off the very set of categories that distinguish early Christian thinking about God in its triadic, yea trinitarian, form.* The proper lens then is not a vertical axis—How divine is Jesus? How divine is the Spirit? Rather, the lens most adequate for early Christian thinking is a web of relations, and once one permits the web to become the paradigm, the relations of the Father, Son, and Spirit come to the fore. One might say, then, that anything like a trinitarian-or-christological monotheism is an expression in need of change to "trinitarian." Once one mutates monotheism, one is in need of another category, and Hill proposes that we do just that.

Does the evidence prohibit doing so because it suggests subordination of the Son to the Father, and does this not speak of something along the vertical axis? This is where Hill's nuances come to the fore, because stopping with subordination does not adequately measure the scope of early Christian claims. As he states it,

---

[23]Wesley Hill, *Paul and the Trinity: Persons, Relations, and the Pauline Letters* (Grand Rapids, MI: Eerdmans, 2015), 168-69, emphasis added.

Two affirmations emerge that call into question the usefulness of the "subordination" rubric. First, God's and Jesus' identities are constituted in and by their differing ways of relating to one another: God sends and exalts, Jesus is sent and exalted. But second, those differing relations are one perspective on God and Jesus that must be held together with a second perspective which sees them as fundamentally one or unified: God and Jesus share the divine name; they are both together "the Lord."[24]

Asymmetry, yes, but not in a way that simply moves up and down on a vertical axis. For the one who is sent in Philippians 2:6-11 is the one who is equal, and the one who dies is the one who has the very name of God. There is no competition or even tension between the high and low in passages like this but instead a mutuality of persons who perform tasks characteristic of that person. The asymmetry is mutually defining, not excluding. That is, what is proper to one is not about essence. Thus there is what Hill sometimes calls "asymmetrical mutuality." To speak of Father is to imply Son, to speak of Son is to imply Father, and to speak of Father or Son is to speak of Spirit, and Spirit implies Father and Son—in Pauline theology.

In short, Hill grabs later theological categories as a heuristic for reading earlier texts, not to impose on them but to ask whether they might be cooperative. They are. He then speaks of the "hermeneutical fruitfulness of trinitarian theology" and "that trinitarian doctrine may be used *retrospectively* to shed light on and enable a deeper penetration of the Pauline texts in their own historical milieu, and that it is not necessarily anachronistic to allow later Christian categories to be the lens through which one reads Paul." Further, "the results of such an endeavor may, it is hoped, lead to further examination of the interdependence of biblical exegesis and dogmatic theology. If trinitarian theology comes to the assistance of the

---

[24]Hill, *Paul and the Trinity*, 170.

exegete grappling with Paul's theology, then that reader of Paul may in turn remind trinitarian theology of its own exegetical roots."[25] This does not make the apostles full-blown trinitarian theologians. Rather, it simultaneously unmasks the hidden implication of bracketing off later categories as it also opens up the possibilities of those later categories. If one does not plumb the relationalities of Father, Son, and Spirit—relationalities already present in the New Testament in abundance—then one will not find a Christology rooted in relationalities. If one decides on a vertical axis, one will be shaped and hampered by that axis.

I could go on, but I want to show how two other scholars have worked New Testament texts in a way that moves beyond what Hill calls the vertical axis and onto a more relational web. Neither of them is as explicit as Hill in using later trinitarian categories in a heuristic manner, but both have in fact demonstrated the hermeneutical fruitfulness of such categories (as Hill is quoted above). What these scholars demonstrate is that New Testament scholars, to be ecclesial theologians, need the theologians of the church in order to map the terrain of the New Testament.

Matthew Bates. The work of the vertical-axis scholars concentrated on texts and practices of the New Testament that suggested the deity of Christ. That focus of their lens missed out on another feature that Matthew Bates has brought into view, namely, the use of the Old Testament in the mode of *prosopological exegesis*.[26] If Wesley Hill has used later categories heuristically to turn New Testament Christology from the vertical axis to a relational web, Bates and Madison Pierce have demonstrated that the relational web is more prominent than perhaps even Hill thinks.

---

[25]Hill, *Paul and the Trinity*, 171.
[26]Matthew W. Bates, *The Hermeneutics of the Apostolic Proclamation: The Center of Paul's Method of Scriptural Interpretation* (Waco, TX: Baylor University Press, 2012); Bates, *The Birth of the Trinity* (Oxford: Oxford University Press, 2016). This section describes what is found in *Birth of the Trinity*.

What is prosopological exegesis? The Greek word *prosopon* means "face" or "person," and prosopological exegesis is to posit unnamed persons speaking in and through Old Testament texts. A classic example is found when Jesus asks the bewildering question in Mark 12:36-37: "David himself, by the Holy Spirit, declared, [David speaking now of] 'The Lord [God, who] said to my Lord [Messiah], "Sit at my right hand, until I put your enemies under your feet."'" If David calls him "Lord," Jesus has asked, "How can the scribes say that the Messiah is the son of David?" (Mk 12:35). Jesus then states the above quotation and asks, "How can he be his son?" (Mk 12:37). The question we ask is, Who is saying what here? The tension we feel as we read this text is the tension they felt, and to relieve that tension they attributed speakers to clarify.

Or, take Hebrews 10:5-7:

Consequently, when Christ came into the world, he said,
    "Sacrifices and offerings you have not desired,
        but a body you have prepared for me;
    in burnt offerings and sin offerings
        you have taken no pleasure.
    Then I said, 'See, God, I have come to do your will, O God'
        (in the scroll of the book it is written of me)."

The author knows it was Christ who said these things to the Father, and he knows this through a reading that is prosopological. The author, for a variety of reasons, attributes the words of a psalm (Ps 40:6; LXX 39:7) to a person (*prosopon*).

Or, Romans 15:1-4, this one using Psalm 68:10 LXX:

We who are strong ought to put up with the failings of the weak, and not to please ourselves. Each of us must please our neighbor for the good purpose of building up the neighbor. *For Christ did not please himself; but, as it is written, "The insults of those who insult you have fallen on me."* For whatever was written in former

days was written for our instruction, so that by steadfastness
and by the encouragement of the scriptures we might have hope.

In the heated contest in the Roman house churches, the weak and the
strong were at one another's throats, and the apostle pulls out his
Christoformity theme and appeals for his basis to a psalm, to whose
words he attributes Christ speaking (set in italics). This, Paul says, shows
how Scriptures can be used and helpful for Christian congregations.

What Bates shows in his book is this: that prosopological exegesis
was Jewish; that Jesus himself participated in such; that the early
Christians did; *and that in their prosopological exegesis a Christology
and trinitarian thinking was not only assumed but visible.* Furthermore,
Bates ponders numerous prosopological exegesis texts in the New
Testament and so explores preexistence, the mission of the Son in
dialogue with the Father, cross-shaped conversations, praise for
rescue, triumphant expectations, and reading God right. The themes
that one finds in this form of early Christian hermeneutic are macro-
scopic. In fact, *Bates contends this person-centered reading of the Old
Testament was the birth of the Trinity, by which he is speaking of the linguistic emergence of Trinity as a theological construct.* This, so it seems
to me, is justifiable. Trinitarian thinking was assumed by prosopological exegesis but at the same expanded it by articulating even
further by reading Father, Son, and Spirit back into the texts that did
not specifically mention them but that begged for their presence.

New Testament scholars, however, have ignored prosopological
exegesis, and to this day many, if not most, oppose it as a legitimate
form of reading the Old Testament. Yet, this is how Jesus and the
apostles read the Bible at times. In exploring prosopological exegesis,
one discovers some of the threads of what later became trinitarian
theology. The vertical-axis scholars have completely ignored it as I
read them. Why? Because we (I include myself) have bracketed off
not only creedal trinitarian thinking but especially the patristic method
of Bible reading. You can't see what you choose not to look at.

Bates is not alone, but he is in the minority. What Bates shows is that by pondering the exegesis of the patristics in light of the later trinitarian thinking, we actually get closer to the hermeneutic and the theology of Jesus and the apostles than we do when we restrict our minds to the historical-critical method and bracket off later thinking. Perhaps the later thinking is in direct line with the New Testament itself.

Madison Pierce. I turn now to Madison Pierce's *Divine Discourse in the Epistle to the Hebrews*, a work that expands Bates's prosopological exegesis into a studied focus of Hebrews that simultaneously sheds light on early trinitarian thinking ignored by vertical-axis thinking (as mentioned above).[27] Along with numerous insights into the letter of Hebrews, Pierce's study of prosopological exegesis does something that Bates only hints at: namely, she comes as close as anyone to the Cappadocians in exploring the mutual interaction between Father and Son and Spirit. She is not exploring social trinitarianism as it has been done, but she does explore the divine speech or discourse of Father, Son, and Spirit. Notice these texts in Hebrews and use them to ponder early Christology and trinitarian thinking.

In Hebrews we encounter (1) the Father who loves the Son speaking (prosopologically) *about* and *to* the Son for all to hear (Heb 1:5-9):

For to which of the angels did God ever say,

> "You are my Son;
> > today I have begotten you"?

Or again,

> "I will be his Father,
> > and he will be my Son"?

And again, when he brings the firstborn into the world, he says,

> "Let all God's angels worship him."

---

[27]Madison N. Pierce, *Divine Discourse in the Epistle to the Hebrews: The Recontextualization of Spoken Quotations of Scripture*, Society for New Testament Studies Monograph Series 178 (New York: Cambridge University Press, 2020).

Of the angels he says,

> "He makes his angels winds,
>> and his servants flames of fire."

But of the Son he says,

> "Your throne, O God, is forever and ever,
>> and the righteous scepter is the scepter of your kingdom.
> You have loved righteousness and hated wickedness;
> therefore God, your God, has anointed you
>> with the oil of gladness beyond your companions."

This Father speaks of the Son in Hebrews 5 and 7 and clarifies even more about the Son's redemption: he is a Son-Priest like Melchizedek whose ministry rests on better promises and forms the new covenant, which the Father announces in Hebrews 8. Pierce shows that in loving the Son the Father loves the children of God.

(2) The Son who serves speaks (prosopologically) in Hebrews 2:11-13, saying:

> For the one who sanctifies and those who are sanctified all have one Father. For this reason Jesus is not ashamed to call them brothers and sisters, saying,
>
>> "I will proclaim your name to my brothers and sisters,
>>> in the midst of the congregation I will praise you."
> And again,
>> "I will put my trust in him."
> And again,
>> "Here am I and the children whom God has given me."

He speaks again in Hebrews 10:5-7, this time to the Father, through being assigned words from the Old Testament (LXX Ps 39:7-9):

> Consequently, when Christ came into the world, he said,
>
>> "Sacrifices and offerings you [God the Father] have not
>>> desired,

> but a body you have prepared for me;
> in burnt offerings and sin offerings
>   you have taken no pleasure.
> Then I said, 'See, God, I have come to do your will, O God'
>   (in the scroll of the book it is written of me)."

We now have Father speaking to Son and Son speaking to Father.

And (3) the Spirit exhorts and admonishes the people of God, and here we take a cue from Hebrews 3:7-11 (as well as through Heb 4:11):[28]

> Therefore, as the Holy Spirit says,
>
> "Today, if you hear his voice,
>   do not harden your hearts as in the rebellion,
>   as on the day of testing in the wilderness,
>   where your ancestors put me to the test,
>   though they had seen my works for forty years.
>   Therefore I was angry with that generation,
>   and I said, 'They always go astray in their hearts,
>   and they have not known my ways.'
>   As in my anger I swore,
>   'They will not enter my rest.'"

It is not possible to entertain the complexities of these texts or all that Pierce brings to the surface, and neither is that my intent in this chapter. Rather, I want to show that the author of Hebrews *perceives* God in three speaking voices, in three *prosopa* if one uses the method to see persons speaking, and in such a manner we find in Hebrews both preexistence of three persons and divine interaction of three persons.

The vertical-axis approach has failed to see the early trinitarian implications of prosopological exegesis. In some ways it is because

---

[28]This has been worked out extensively for the pre-Nicene period in a way that could influence biblical studies more by Kyle R. Hughes, *The Trinitarian Testimony of the Spirit: Prosopological Exegesis and the Development of Pre-Nicene Pneumatology*, Supplements to Vigiliae Christianae 147 (Leiden: Brill, 2018); Hughes, *How the Spirit Became God: The Mosaic of Early Christian Pneumatology* (Eugene, OR: Cascade, 2020).

such scholarship operates with the blinder of the historical-critical method, with the intentional choice of bracketing out the later trinitarian categories, and in so doing sees only what it can see by its method. But scholars such as Pierce, by learning from later methods and therefore later categories, illuminate not only early Christology but a path forward to show that New Testament scholars need to expand their vision and listen to later voices who can provide categories that may help understand the New Testament itself. She observes that "the use of this technique" in Hebrews "is ubiquitous and methodical and exceptional."[29] Noticeably, Jesus speaks more in Hebrews, and only in Hebrews does the Spirit speak. We have what she calls divine discourse on display in Hebrews.

What we have seen in these three New Testament exegetes—Hill, Bates, Pierce—is fair-minded New Testament scholarship that is interacting with theology more often connected to the later church. But they are pressing us to ask whether it is as late as many (e.g., Dunn) have led us to think. I think not.

INTEGRATING OUR DISCIPLINES

Two observations now from theologian Robert Jenson. First, these prosopological studies especially (Bates, Pierce) take us a step closer to how Jenson defines *person* in his modification of Boethius: "a person is one with whom other persons—the circularity is constitutive —can *converse*, whom they can *address*."[30] As the persons speak to and are spoken to in these prosopological studies, and as Wesley Hill points to relationality, so Jenson: personhood is fundamentally relational/communicational.[31] Thus Jenson operates his trinitarian theology of person with a *communicative* sense rather than a *possessed*

---

[29]Pierce, *Divine Discourse*, 201.

[30]Jenson, *Systematic Theology* 1:117.

[31]Sarah Coakley's Spirit-directed incorporative model of our relationship with God, versus a hierarchical, linear, and vertical model, complements these observations. See Coakley, *God, Sexuality, and the Self.*

sense. Theologians need to know we New Testament scholars need to think more in terms of persons like Jenson.

Second, Jenson opens his chapter "Of One Being with the Father" with these provocative words: "'The doctrine of the Trinity' is less a homogenous body of propositions than it is a task." And what might that task be? "That of the church's continuing effort to recognize and adhere to the biblical God's hypostatic being." After sketching some relational expressions in the New Testament, he offers this: "Christians [who follow the logic of the New Testament itself] can live only in a dramatic and linguistic space determined by the coordinates of the triune name: to the Father, with the Son, in the Spirit."[32]

It is not uncommon for systematicians to make strong claims about what the Bible says and then hear biblical scholars say "but, but, but," and some of those buts have been heard already in this chapter. But the final examples of this chapter are suggesting that Jenson's claim has more in its favor than earlier examples were prepared to give it. That he can conclude his first volume by saying God is a "fugue" brings into a metaphor what these biblical scholars are getting at: Father, Son, Spirit conversing, and we, God's people, taking in the music of the divine conversation.[33]

But at times the theologians can go too far. In the next chapter I will examine how theology at times jumps the rails and requires Bible folks to bring them back in line. Before we get there, I want to contextualize the findings of the first two chapters. If our God is Trinity, then it means God is a God in relations (Father, Son, Spirit). If we can say, then, that the persons of God are communicants one with another, then we have to see that Scripture—the focus of this book—is the communication of the Communicating One to humans who can communicate with God. We can then say that

---

[32]Jenson, *Systematic Theology* 1:90, 93-94.

[33]Jenson, *Systematic Theology* 1:236. Some dimensions of Jenson's trinitarian theology have been challenged in Scott R. Swain, *The God of the Gospel: Robert Jenson's Trinitarian Theology* (Downers Grove, IL: IVP Academic, 2013).

Scripture is communicants communicating with communicants. That, in itself, changes what we are doing when we do biblical theology, and it calls theologians to Scripture as it calls biblical theologians to listen to the theologians.

THEOLOGY NEEDS HISTORICALLY SHAPED BIBLICAL STUDIES

PERHAPS THE PLACE TO BEGIN this chapter is with the observation that sometimes biblical and systematic studies become wildly out of sync and are in need of coordination if they are not to become isolated disciplines. Neither discipline remains the same, each is growing, but if the growth patterns are not recognized and incorporated into each other, each loses its way in the pursuit of fuller truth. Some in my field believe theology needs to listen to us while it is not our responsibility to pay attention to them. This kind of patronizing of the other is simply not respected by the systematicians, and we need to develop a more amenable form of discourse. If there is too much anarchist impulse in biblical studies, there is too little exegesis and historical context in systematics.

In broaching the up-to-date developments in each discipline here we run the risk of excluding the other. It is not uncommon for a Bible scholar to begin an essay and even a monograph by admitting she hasn't been able to read everything, and sometimes affixed to this is the admission that adjacent fields have been more or less ignored . . . and the same pertains to systematics. So, let me say it clearly: if we biblical specialists cannot become aware of even all the best studies in our own disciplines, we cannot expect systematicians to come close to being aware of all that is going on in our field, which is why we need one another, which is why the previous chapter came before this chapter.

Biblical studies are ideally exegesis in context, and that means a recognition of numerous contexts, specialists in each area, arcane publications abounding, and the need to listen to such studies to discern a reasonable understanding of the text in context, whether it is ancient Near Eastern studies about creation stories, various anthropological and historically situated studies of sacrifice and atonement, the nature of ancient culture's political authorities and governance, the development of Judaism from ancient Israel into early rabbinics, the Dead Sea Scrolls and their impact in many directions, and all this recontextualized yet again as the apostles moved out from the land of Israel into the Roman Empire, where they imbibed and adjusted and challenged both Greek and Roman cultures. All this and more is involved in biblical studies, and it requires hard work to comprehend the conversations.

Recognizing historical context matters because everything has a context. It is boilerplate to say that a text apart from a context is a pretext but it's still true—both then and now. If I say "taxation," you say . . . what? What you say will be shaped by your context of meaning, and what I hear you say will be shaped by mine. It is a fact that many statements about what the Bible says are derived from contextless exegeses of a former generation. I've been researching the book of Revelation recently. Comparing what many evangelical Christians believe about future eschatology (rapture, millennium, the intermediate state, etc.), the deposit of previous generations of scholarship becomes evident, some of which are permanently solid, while others are vaporous. Our Bible is not like the Book of Mormon, for which it is claimed that it dropped from the sky somehow and was more or less contextless. The Christian Bible is a long narrative stretching over millennia with shifting contexts, but that Bible witnesses to a God who acted and spoke at specific moments to specific people in specific situations. Thus, our revelation is contextual and historically bound, and any theological claim rooted in texts from another culture will need to demonstrate a sensitive listening to that text in its context. So much, then, for the big picture and the theory.

BIBLICAL STUDIES VALUABLE FOR SYSTEMATIC THEOLOGY: FOUR RECENT WORKS

Time will tell whether systematicians will pay close enough attention to the widespread and continually deepening work of John ("Jack") Levison on the Spirit in the Old Testament and Judaism. Levison has been pointing out for years that New Testament scholars and systematicians see the Hebrew word "spirit" (*ruach*) connected to the word *God* in the Old Testament and immediately use the uppercase *Spirit*, and there we have it: trinitarian theology! Levison, in careful, cautious, and long-term exegeses in context, shows that this Hebrew term points us to wind, breath, spirit as in "human spirit" and to Spirit as in "divine Spirit." Fine. The problem is that while some are easily distinguishable, many uses in the Old Testament aren't. There are nearly four hundred uses of this term in the Old Testament, and there is *considerable overlap*, and one sometimes (or more often than that) can't distinguish human spirit from divine Spirit, and *this may be instructive and constructive* for systematic theology. Levison's work deserves careful consideration by systematicians, and it could well produce a new kind of *ruach*-ology that reshapes or at least contributes to our pneumatology.[1] Theologian Robert Jenson too easily slips from

---

[1] John R. Levison, *Filled with the Spirit* (Grand Rapids, MI: Eerdmans, 2009); Levison, *Inspired: The Holy Spirit and the Mind of Faith* (Grand Rapids, MI: Eerdmans, 2013); Levison, *The Holy Spirit Before Christianity* (Waco, TX: Baylor University Press, 2019); Levison, *Boundless God: The Spirit According to the Old Testament* (Grand Rapids, MI: Baker Academic, 2020).

breath to uppercase *Spirit* in his brief overview of the persons of God's identity as well as in his more substantial chapter on the Spirit.[2]

New Testament studies continues its steady march into new discoveries and fresh insights, many of which could be of use to the systematician. A study that pertains more to political theology than to the classic topics of systematic theology is the wonderful work of American Indian New Testament scholar Christopher Hoklotubbe on the meaning of *eusebeia* in the Pastoral Epistles.[3] In his wideranging study Hoklotubbe shows that this term is commonly translated "godliness" or a "godly life" in the Pastorals (e.g., 1 Tim 2:2; 4:7-8; 6:3, 5-6, 11; 2 Tim 3:5; Titus 1:1 [NRSV, NIV]). But the term *godliness* has connotations that suggest "being godlike." It evokes the history of discussion about sanctification and separation, and even has at times boundary-marking behaviors: To take an example, one says, "He's a godly teacher," and that means someone else is not. Hoklotubbe, however, proves beyond any doubt that this term means something like "civilized piety" and evokes not separation but social respect and cultural respectability. That is, it marks not the person unlike society but the one who fits into society in a way that does not bring disrespect to culture or to the church. Furthermore, Hoklotubbe makes it clear this term describes a Christian appropriation of a common expression for a Christian way of life that makes a good impression in public life. To repeat, this does not shift systematics in a measurable way, but it does provoke us to think differently about political theology and Christian ethics. Unquestionably this is the kind of contribution to scholarship that I would argue systematicians need to become alert to and somehow to incorporate into their work. New Testament studies are moving all the time, and no one can keep up, but each of us needs to work with others to enhance all of our disciplines.

---

[2]Robert W. Jenson, *Systematic Theology* (New York: Oxford University Press, 1997), 1:86-88, 146-61.

[3]T. Christopher Hoklotubbe, *Civilized Piety: The Rhetoric of Pietas in the Pastoral Epistles and the Roman Empire* (Waco, TX: Baylor University Press, 2017).

I mention now only a few studies in passing. Susan Eastman, in her study of anthropology in *Paul and the Person*, demonstrates that humans are fundamentally dyadic and not monadic.[4] That is, our identity is formed in relationship to others and not simply as individuals. This affects, of course, how one frames both Christian ethics and ecclesiology, but it also calls our attention to the individualistic theologies produced by theologians (and biblical scholars) who may well be thinking they are thinking on their own. One's self is formed in relation to others—subject and object are not as distinguishable.[5] Matthew Croasmun's *The Emergence of Sin* is a wide-ranging study that explores the so-called personification of sin in Romans and shows that emergence theory presses us into recognizing Sin as an *agent*. The supervenience of individual human sins over time, then, form into the agent Sin, which depends on the supervenience basis but expands it into something alive and which then has downward causation to influence the individual to sin more and more. What happens, I ask in brief, to our soteriology when the sins we commit are at least in part shaped by the agent Sin at work in our world?[6]

One final example, one that I have been involved in: the meaning of *gospel*. The gospel, truth be told, has been so narrated into Western Christianity's worldview that it is almost ecumenical to think the Four Spiritual Laws or the Bridge or some variant of those, nuances aside, is the gospel: God loves us, we are sinners, Jesus died for us, we need only trust him, and we go to heaven when we die. The focus has been on the crucifixion, with a decided lack of emphasis of the resurrection, and one atonement theory (penal substitution) was very influential

---

[4]Susan Grove Eastman, *Paul and the Person: Reframing Paul's Anthropology* (Grand Rapids, MI: Eerdmans, 2017).

[5]Eastman, *Paul and the Person.*

[6]Matthew Croasmun, *The Emergence of Sin: The Cosmic Tyrant in Romans* (New York: Oxford University Press, 2017).

in the substance of the gospel and its appeal.[7] One of the appeals of N. T. Wright's decades-long battle with the heaven aspect of many understandings of the gospel is that it has pushed many to take a new look at the meaning of *gospel*. To make a long story short, I happened upon studying the gospel itself through teaching undergraduates and giving lectures in various places, and that study convinced me that I had been wrong in that gospel I describe above, which I call the soterian gospel, and that the gospel of the apostles was a different framing from the soterian framing. I wrote this up in *The King Jesus Gospel*, in the second edition of which I developed a chapter that traced (at least the widespread attractiveness of) the soterian gospel to Billy Graham's evangelistic crusades. What I discovered is nothing other than seeing what was there all along that I had not seen. I was personally thrilled that a young scholar, Matthew Bates, joined me in challenging evangelicalism's trench-deep commitment to the soterian approach.[8] When one adds to this perception of gospel Bates's development of Teresa Morgan's challenges about the meaning of faith as allegiance, there are suddenly new challenges for theologians to think how the gospel is being framed in systematics.

These examples are more parochial compared to the major example I want to focus on in this chapter.

REFRAMED GRACE: EXPLORING BARCLAY'S IMPACT

Sometimes the footings of systematics are dislodged and relocated by rigorous historical biblical scholarship, and, if the theologians don't

---

[7]Robert Jenson has much less emphasis on crucifixion, as his emphasis is on resurrection, so that the God of the Trinity is the God who raised Jesus from the dead (*Systematic Theology* 1:179-93). Noteworthy as a statement is this from him: "The Crucifixion is God's salvific action just in that God overcomes it by the Resurrection" (1:182). The resurrection thus is God's word that the crucifixion reveals the kind of God that God actually is (1:189).

[8]Scot McKnight, *The King Jesus Gospel: The Original Good News Revisited*, 2nd ed. (Grand Rapids, MI: Zondervan, 2015); Matthew W. Bates, *Salvation by Allegiance Alone: Rethinking Faith, Works, and the Gospel of Jesus the King* (Grand Rapids, MI: Baker Academic, 2017); Bates, *Gospel Allegiance* (Grand Rapids, MI: Brazos, 2019).

adjust, they end up building a house on loose or even nonexistent footings. A recent study of grace in the ancient world has shifted the footings considerably—in some ways widened the footings, in some cases formed entirely new footings, and in other ways challenged systematicians' view of grace itself. That study is by John Barclay, who has made the bold but not polemically shaped claim that no one has really studied Paul's theology of grace found in Pauline theology.[9] Barclay's view of grace has challenged the adequacy of the commonly defined view of grace and should give a generation of systematicians new ground on which to work.

For many years I used a collection of definitions of grace found at Christianity.com as illustrations of how grace was understood in the Protestant (and Reformed) traditions, but when Barclay's *Paul and the Gift* was published, it was clear we were in need of a revised definition. I will begin here with this set of standard definitions from recognizable thinkers before getting to Barclay's study, which challenges systematic theories of grace.

Grace in common understandings. So, how is grace understood in the Christian tradition, and what definition is operative in Christian theology shaped by these definitions?

B. B. Warfield: "Grace is free sovereign favor to the ill-deserving."

Jerry Bridges: "[Grace] is God reaching downward to people who are in rebellion against Him."

Paul Zahl: "Grace is unconditional love toward a person who does not deserve it."

Wayne Grudem: "God's 'grace' means his 'unmerited favor.'" Or in another location, "God's grace means God's goodness toward those who deserve only punishment."[10]

---

[9]John M. G. Barclay, *Paul and the Gift* (Grand Rapids, MI: Eerdmans, 2015).
[10]Justin Holcomb, "What Is Grace?," Christianity.com, www.christianity.com/theology/what-is-grace.html. I have added Wayne Grudem.

To deepen these definitions, I turn to Gerald Bray's definition of grace in the *New Dictionary of Theology*.[11] Bray himself opens with a common-sounding definition: "In its primary meaning, grace is undeserved favour, usually that extended from a superior to an inferior." The emphasis in each of these definitions, and not the fuller study of each, is God's condescending love for humans, who are sinners and undeserving of that love. Notice these terms in the above definitions: "ill-deserving" and "people who are in rebellion" and "does not deserve it" and "those who deserve only punishment" and "superior to an inferior." In Barclay's list of perfections, discussed below, each of these definitions above emphasizes the *incongruity* of God's grace, and both Barclay and each of these theologians get that right. Humans are undeserving of God's grace. We must ask already: Are these adequate definitions? I think not.

Bray, sorting out a history of grace in theology with almost no emphasis on the Bible's own theology (!), thinks the doctrine of grace was not developed in the church until Augustine, but it would be more accurate to say that the Augustinian theory of grace was not developed until Augustine, for, again as Barclay shows, grace was fully at work in Judaism as well as the Greco-Roman world.[12] Augustine, Bray explains, saw grace in comprehensive terms: it was prevenient, cooperative, sufficient, and efficient. In short, all of redemption is all of grace. A departure is found in the medieval scholastics, where grace was administered through various means (church, prayer, sacraments) but in a distinctive way was added on to nature itself, and Bray thinks the nature-grace dualism (from Aristotle) that filtered through medieval theology precipitated in important ways the Reformation of the sixteenth

---

[11]Gerald L. Bray, "Grace," in *New Dictionary of Theology*, 2nd ed., ed. Martin Davie et al. (Downers Grove, IL: IVP Academic, 2016), 376-78. All citations are from these three pages.

[12]For a dense condensation of the Bible's various expressions, see Anthony C. Thiselton, *The Thiselton Companion to Christian Theology* (Grand Rapids, MI: Eerdmans, 2015), 386-91. On my remark about Bray, the *New Dictionary of Theology's* assignment was to focus on the historical and systematic topics, illustrating the very problem this book is attempting to sort out, namely, the dialectical relationship of Bible and theology.

century. Protestantism, Bray contends, shifted the means of grace to preaching the gospel. How grace was understood split theologians in Calvinist and Arminian directions, and the former built a theology of grace that operated on more than one level. Those levels include a covenant of works and common grace with all humans, and a covenant of grace (special grace) for the elect, beginning with Abraham.

John Barclay's definitions and perfections. Barclay's *Paul and the Gift* is one of the most significant books in New Testament studies in the past century. Barclay's study is multidisciplinary and examines how *gift* and *gift exchange* were understood in anthropology, in the Greco-Roman world of gift exchange and mutual reciprocity with its social network, and in the history of Christian theology (where for some it has come to mean "pure gift," which is operative in many understandings of grace). Furthermore, Barclay is a world-class scholar of all things Pauline, and his *Paul and the Gift* is nothing if not an equal-opportunity critic. His approach is never polemical, but he does point to the lacks in scholarship. In effect, he shows that no study of grace has been accomplished the way it should have been done, and in part this is because we think we have grace down and our theology keeps us in place. What is noticeable about the studies above, to take but one example, is the total absence of "gift" expressions and thus of something like spiritual gifts. What Barclay does is expose our theology of grace to the ancient world—Jewish, Greek, Roman—in such a way to expose as well the foundations of our theology of grace.[13]

Barclay knows that grace and gift are part of the social system of the Roman Empire, so all of a sudden there are new dimensions to what *grace* means in Paul. His definition takes us to a new level:

"Gift" denotes the sphere of *voluntary, personal relations, charac-terized by goodwill in the giving of benefit or favor, and eliciting some form of reciprocal return that is both voluntary and necessary*

---

[13]E.g., Kevin DeYoung, *Grace Defined and Defended: What a Four-Hundred-Year-Old Confession Teaches Us About Sin, Salvation, and the Sovereignty of God* (Wheaton, IL: Crossway, 2019).

for the continuation of the relationship. In accord with the anthropology of gift, its scope includes various forms of kindness, favor, generosity, or compassion enacted in diverse services and benefits, with the expectation of some reciprocating gratitude or counter-gift. Ancient languages articulate this field of relations in a rich variety of terms, which often overlap in meaning but may also contain subtly different connotations.[14]

This concluding definition emerges from this study as a way to correct word books and lexicons. Barclay's comprehensive study of anthropology, social history, and theological development leads to the following conclusions, and here the potency for theology of these various conclusions becomes obvious:

(i) gifts are generally given in order to create or reproduce social bonds; they foster mutuality, and for this reason are typically neither unilateral nor anonymous;

(ii) the rules of reciprocity raise the expectation of return, even in unequal social relations and even if the return is generally different from the gift in quantity and kind;

(iii) the recipient of the gift is under a strong though non-legal obligation to reciprocate;

(iv) the gift is often associated with the person of the giver, and is therefore, to some degree, "inalienable";

(v) reflecting this personal investment, gifts are usually construed as voluntary and expressive of goodwill, even if they arise from pre-existing bonds of obligation;

(vi) thus, gifts and counter-gifts may be both voluntary and obligatory at the same time, and similarly both "interested" and "disinterested." The scrambling of these categories does not cohere with modern concepts of "altruism," "the pure gift," and "the gift without strings."[15]

---

[14]Barclay, *Paul and the Gift*, 575.
[15]Barclay, *Paul and the Gift*, 183-84.

Thus, all in italics: *"The difference between an incongruous and a congruous gift is a difference in one perfection of grace, not a categorical distinction between grace and non-grace."*[16]

Perhaps the most important set of categories in Barclay's groundbreaking work is his pointing out six perfections (one could call them themes as well) of grace. This expression, "perfections of grace," focuses on "the tendency to draw the theme of gift/grace to an end-of-the-line extreme, especially for polemical purposes and in relation to God; and we have observed the variety of forms that this 'perfecting' tendency can take."[17] When not taken to their extreme, these various terms are themes or elements or features of grace and gift discourse. Barclay's six perfections are, first, *superabundance*: when the descriptions move in the direction of scale, extravagance, and permanence of the gift given. Second, *singularity*: when the descriptions focus on the giver, in our case God the Giver of the gift, as marked by grace or giving at all times. Thus perfected, one would speak of God as not capable of but giving and forgiving. Third, *priority*: when the description emphasizes the giver's initiative and giving before anything else could happen. To glance at Pauline scholarship, the emphasis of E. P. Sanders's emphasis on Israel and Judaism being marked by grace is that the covenant preceded the law, so that covenant equals grace and grace is prior to the law, so all of Judaism is rooted in God's grace. Fourth, *incongruity*: when the descriptions shape the discourse about grace, with emphasis on the giver's superior status and the recipient's inferior status or unworthy status, or, in theological terms, on God's utter holiness and the human's utter sinfulness. Fifth, *efficacy*: when the description of the giving of a gift turns toward the nature and agency of the recipient, and one might say the impact transforms or reforms or reshapes the recipient into one obligated and allegiant to the giver of the gift. Sixth, *noncircularity*: grace is perfected at times

---

[16]Barclay, *Paul and the Gift*, 317.
[17]Barclay, *Paul and the Gift*, 185.

when it becomes pure gift. That is, when the giver gives and the recipient does nothing and can do nothing in return. This understanding of grace is, again, common among those who stereotype grace in Christian theology and is at work in more than the Reformed camps. Those quick to pull out the semi-Pelagian accusation often camp out in this sixth perfection. What Barclay shows is that actually very few theologians in history affirmed noncircularity. His own study of grace and gift in the ancient world demonstrates unequivocally that gift giving drew the recipient into a social bond, into a relationship, that obligated the recipient to mutual reciprocity. It's perhaps too crass to put this way, but in most discussions of grace and gift in the ancient world, nothing was free. Pure gift, then, cannot be assumed when the Bible communicates grace and gift.

We are at a turning point here in understanding grace, not only in the ancient world but in what that means for theology and how this sound historical study now rearranges some of the ways (as illustrated above in their inadequacies) theology itself is done. First, most operative ideas about grace are rooted in Augustine and Luther, and even New Testament scholars assume those two giants got grace right. Second, grace is understood (or perfected) in some ways by one group and in other ways by other groups. It is just as inaccurate to say Judaism's works gave way to Christian grace as it is to say Pelagius or Arminians or Catholics have no sense of grace while the Reformed or Puritans or Baptists do. What the Reformed perfect may not be what Catholics do, but grace has various perfections. Barclay's work proves that we must be more attentive to the nuances of grace, and thus we must perceive Paul comparatively:

> Paul's relation to Second Temple Judaism should not be confined to two current but overly simplistic options: either Paul advocated grace against a grace-less and "legalistic" Judaism, or Paul was in full agreement with all his fellow Jews on the character of

grace. We may start with a simpler question: *how do Paul's perfec-tions of grace compare with those of his fellow Jews?*[18]

Barclay's own work makes it abundantly clear that there's no dimin-ishment of Paul's emphasis on the incongruity of grace: humans are undeserving, status doesn't matter; God's grace is prior and super-abundant. But these perfections of grace, too, lead to another im-portant conclusion: grace cannot be reduced to a single meaning or core characteristic because grace has various significances, and grace is not better the more perfections are added. In addition, different contexts call forth different elements of this multiphasic sense of grace.

Hence, after his careful study of grace in Judaism, Barclay draws the threads together into a summary that should shock how Christian theologians have spoken about the absence of grace in Judaism:

> Using the sixfold schema of perfections described . . . , we have found that our texts agree at some points, and differ widely at others. *All of them* perfect the superabundance of divine "grace," stressing the excess of gifts poured into the world, or the "abun-dance" of divine mercy and goodness, extended in manifold ways. On the other hand, in another point of agreement, *none of them* perfect the non-circularity of grace, the notion that God gives without expectation of return.[19]

This is perhaps the cutting edge of Barclay's study of grace for in-forming systematic theologies of salvation, grace, and faith: grace and duty or grace and reciprocation by a human to God's grace are not mutually exclusive.

While this description of Barclay has grown quite lengthy, I am not yet done because it is important to see where this study leads when it reaches Paul, a Jew, a Christian, and the grace theologian of all grace theologians. First, a general observation: *Paul's grace theology is*

---

[18]Barclay, *Paul and the Gift*, 187.
[19]Barclay, *Paul and the Gift*, 314.

typical and distinctive. Second, the core grace event is Christ—who he is, his sending by the Father, and his life, death, burial, resurrection, and ascension to the throne of God—who launched a universalistic vision of grace for all. Third, which of the perfections did Paul perfect? For Barclay, when the perfections appear in Paul, he seems to perfect only incongruity, and in this Barclay's emphasis was taken up especially by the Reformed. Yet, grace is not complete in Paul with the perfection of incongruity: grace for Paul is paradoxically unconditioned but not unconditional, and Pauline scholars have long observed that one can be in Paul both justified without works and only judged by works. There is, then, a strong emphasis here on the efficacy of grace in Pauline theology. Terms aside, Barclay's own words are what is needed in this discussion: the grace of God encounters the sinful human in an incongruous manner, and the incongruity converts into a kind of congruity, a kind of human whose works measure grace.[20]

Where are we on grace? Barclay's study reveals that the notion of pure gift—noncircular—is neither what Paul is presenting, nor is it the place to begin. First, the place to begin theologizing about grace is with gift giving in human realities and how those realities give rise to a theology or philosophy of gift, grace, and reciprocation. To be sure, each context reshapes gift and grace, but what is clear about Paul is that God is the giver, humans are the recipients, and the humans receiving this gift are turned into agents of grace. The notion then that it is pure gift fails because it jumps the gun.

Second, Barclay shows that grace in Paul perfects the theme of incongruity, but Paul's theology of grace includes priority, superabundance, and the paradoxical efficacy of grace itself. Third, grace in Paul transcends soteriology, which has been the darling location for much Christian theology. Yes, soteriology is central, but for Paul grace begins in God's love, God's holiness, and God's justice, which

---

[20]Barclay, *Paul and the Gift*, 328, 445-46, 491-92, 517, 557-58.

flows into a way of justifying the unjustifiable and redeeming the irredeemable—those who were "not my people" become "my people," to reuse the language of Hosea 1. Grace begins in theology proper and flows into soteriology but then takes life—because gift giving entails social bonds and mutuality and reciprocity—in what has been classically called sanctification and ecclesiology. The recipients of grace, then, become agents of grace in a Pauline theology of grace. They are made worthy of grace by grace itself, and by grace taking on life in their own habitus.

Grace in New Testament studies attuned to the meaning of grace in its contexts, then, has cracked some barriers of grace theology among systematicians and deserves new life to create theology anew. Grace is but one example, and in the next chapter I turn to another example: the importance of narrative giving shape to theology. When theology itself is framed by narrative, theology transcends the traditional topics and becomes more consistently Christian and Jewish and thus biblical.

THEOLOGY NEEDS MORE NARRATIVE

SOME FIFTEEN YEARS AGO I wanted to read more in the history of theology—more accurately, the history of Christian theological reflection or systematics. I asked a theologian friend where to begin, and he suggested to read some theology in chronological order and to begin in the early church with Irenaeus's *On the Apostolic Preaching*. What struck me about Irenaeus's work was that he opens the book with a long narrative of how the Old Testament prepared for redemption in Christ. One could call what Irenaeus wrote a narrative theology, which then can be contrasted with a more systematic approach to theology, as one sees, for instance, in Augustine's *Enchiridion*, which frames an introduction to Christian thought in more philosophical categories.

One thinks, as well, of our creed, whether the Apostles' Creed or the Niceno-Constantinopolitan Creed, which organizes Christian thought and what Christians (are to) believe in three categories: God (the Father), the Son, and the Spirit (with other topics attached to

Spirit). Three articles, three themes, but nonetheless this three-theme approach to what we believe was so influential that we now frame Christian theology in what is called *topoi*, or topics:

- God
- Man (Humans)
- Christ
- Sin
- Salvation
- Ecclesiology
- Eschatology

To this list some, and some don't, add ethics. It really does amaze more than charismatics that the Spirit isn't a separable topic. Still, the two major framing devices for organizing Christian theology are the creed and the topics.

THREE-ARTICLE OR CREEDAL FRAMES

The classic creed of the Christian faith is the Niceno-Constantinopolitan Creed, and it has historically been seen as being organized by three articles, each of which is italicized:

We believe in one God,
the Father, the Almighty,
maker of heaven and earth,
of all that is, seen and unseen.
We believe in one Lord, Jesus Christ,
the only Son of God,
eternally begotten of the Father,
God from God, Light from Light,
true God from true God,
begotten, not made,
of one Being with the Father.

Through him all things were made.
For us and for our salvation
he came down from heaven:
by the power of the Holy Spirit
he became incarnate from the Virgin Mary,
and was made man.
For our sake he was crucified under Pontius Pilate;
he suffered death and was buried.
On the third day he rose again
in accordance with the Scriptures;
he ascended into heaven
and is seated at the right hand of the Father.
He will come again in glory to judge the living and the dead,
and his kingdom will have no end.
We believe in the Holy Spirit, the Lord, the giver of life,
who proceeds from the Father and the Son.
With the Father and the Son he is worshiped and glorified.
He has spoken through the Prophets.
We believe in one holy catholic and apostolic Church.
We acknowledge one baptism for the forgiveness of sins.
We look for the resurrection of the dead,
and the life of the world to come. Amen.

Augustine, to return to my earlier comment, in his *Enchiridion* or catechism manual, organized the topics of theology, the Christian faith,
by the three articles of the creed: (1) faith in God the Creator; (2) faith
in Christ the Redeemer; (3) faith in the Holy Spirit and the church, to
which he adds (4) faith and the forgiveness of sins and (5) faith in the
resurrection and life everlasting, and finishes with sections on hope
and charity (or love).[1] There is also a splendid orientation in Augustine's

---

[1] I use the categories here from the following edition, which itself is rooted in standard scholarship about Augustine: Augustine, *The Augustine Catechism: The Enchiridion on Faith, Hope,
and Charity*, trans. Bruce Harbert (Hyde Park, NY: New City Press, 2008).

catechism on the Christian virtues of faith, hope, and love, which provides a map for the three-article orientation to the Christian faith.

Using the three articles of the creed for framing Christian belief
has a long and noble history and after Augustine (perhaps earlier, I
don't know) for more than a millennium, finding one of its highlights
in the *Summa Theologica* of Thomas Aquinas, the three articles shaped
theology. John Calvin's *Institutes of the Christian Religion* has been, if
not *the*, at least one of the most influential books in Christian theology.[2] Famously, Calvin has four books to his theology: (1) the
knowledge of God the Creator; (2) the knowledge of God the Redeemer in Christ, first disclosed to the fathers under the law and then
to us in the gospel; (3) the way in which we receive the grace of Christ:
what benefits come to us from it, and what effects follow; and (4) the
external means of aids by which God invites us into the society of
Christ and holds us therein. The third book concerns faith and the
Christian life, while the fourth book is about the church. The first two
books are the from the three articles of the creed but then shift into
soteriology in an expansive sense and ecclesiology.

A creedal-framing approach to theology comes from one of the late
twentieth and early twenty-first centuries' most influential theologians,
Robert Jenson.[3] Jenson's systematic theology is more or less a three-
article approach, as he explores a theology of the Trinity and a trinitarian theology, with emphasis on the identity of God in the revelation
of God in Christ (the gospel). The second volume concerns the works
of God, by which Jenson means creation, humans (image of God,
politics and sex, personhood, sin, God's speech in creation), the church,
and the fulfillment (promise, Last Judgment, the great transformation,
the saints, and the telos). Instead of framing Trinity by what we know

---

[2]John Calvin, *Institutes of the Christian Religion*, 2 vols., trans. Ford Lewis Battles, ed. John
T. McNeill, Library of Christian Classics 20-21 (Philadelphia: Westminster, 1960). See also
Bruce Gordon, *John Calvin's Institutes of the Christian Religion: A Biography*, Lives of Great
Religious Books (Princeton, NJ: Princeton University Press, 2016).

[3]Robert W. Jenson, *Systematic Theology*, 2 vols. (New York: Oxford University Press, 1997).

about God, Jenson says we know God in the Christian tradition only as Trinity—who identifies himself not only by but with the exodus and resurrection. Hence, the classic separation of God from soteriology ends as soteriology is fused with God as who God is.

Such a creedal framing of Christian theology has formed and continues to form the church, and one cannot dispute either its forming power or the power that framing has in shaping the minds of Christians.[4] Yet the frame still needs to be supplemented. For now I move to the second framing, the topics.

TOPICS FRAMES

One of the more influential theologians in Western theology, and a foundation-forming theology for Reformed theologians, was Charles Hodge.[5] What distinguished Hodge's theology was its emphasis on inductive, scientific method, and so he opens with a chapter on method, and in his introduction opposes rationalism, mysticism, and Roman Catholicism as he proposes a Protestant rule of faith. He then sorts out Christian theology by starting with theology proper or God (with emphasis on knowing God by revelation, the attributes of God, the Trinity, the divinity of Christ, the decrees of God, creation, providence, miracles, and angels), and then anthropology (origin and nature of humankind, origin of the soul, unity of the human race, the original state of humanity, covenant of works, the fall, sin, and free agency). Part three is about soteriology (the plan of salvation, covenant of grace, person of Christ, the mediatorial work of Christ, the prophetic office, the priestly office, satisfaction of Christ, the extent of the atonement and theories of atonement, intercession of Christ, kingly office of Christ, humiliation and exaltation of Christ, vocation, regeneration, faith, justification, sanctification, law, and means of

[4]Henri de Lubac, *Christian Faith: An Essay on the Structure of the Apostles' Creed*, trans. Brother Richard Arnandez (San Francisco: Ignatius, 1986).
[5]Charles Hodge, *Systematic Theology*, 3 vols. (Grand Rapids, MI: Eerdmans, 1960).

grace), and then part four concerns eschatology (the soul after death, resurrection, second advent, and the "concomitants of the second advent" [general resurrection, final judgment, etc.]).

Many Christians have a biblicistic, prooftext-ish approach to Christian theology and so want theology organized by topics with Bible references and summaries that put into shape "what the Bible teaches about such-and-such." For decades this approach was performed by Augustus Hopkins Strong, who paved the way for all those who love the possibilities of a commonplace book.[6] When I was a college student I acquired a copy of Strong and used it for years as a go-to source for topics, the texts connected to those topics, and quotations. No one book has done this more than Wayne Grudem's *Systematic Theology*. Grudem was a New Testament professor before he became a systematic theology professor, and he went to work replacing older studies that had provided a service of collecting Bible verses, often called proof-texting, under specific themes or topics.[7] Grudem's systematics text has been reprinted time and time again for more than twenty-five years and has been used throughout the homeschool and Christian school movements, and by many pastors as a resource. Grudem has the following topics: Word of God, God, man, Christ and the Holy Spirit, the application of redemption, the church, and the future.

I am about to turn to the impact of biblical scholarship's narrative turn, but before doing so I want to call attention to a recent evangelical, mostly Reformed theology that is as three-article as it is topical in frame, yet these are reframed by his gospel narrative. Here I refer to Australian Michael Bird.[8] Like almost the whole theological tradition, Bird begins with how we talk about God, and one of his major

---

[6]Augustus Strong, *Systematic Theology: A Compendium and Common-Place Book for the Use of Theological Students* (Philadelphia: Judson, 1907). On commonplace books, see Ann Moss, *Printed Commonplace-Books and the Structuring of Renaissance Thought* (New York: Clarendon, 1996).

[7]Wayne Grudem, *Systematic Theology*, 2nd ed. (Grand Rapids, MI: Zondervan, 2020).

[8]Michael F. Bird, *Evangelical Theology: A Biblical and Systematic Introduction*, 2nd ed. (Grand Rapids, MI: Zondervan, 2020).

contributions is that his theology is gospel-driven, or what I might call gospel-framed. For some *gospel* has become a buzzword, but Bird's perception of gospel has been informed by recent studies on gospel, and it's not a rehash of Billy Graham's gospel of personal salvation.[9] Bird has chapters on the God of the gospel (the triune God), the gospel of the kingdom (gospel, kingdom, now and not yet, the future, etc.), the gospel of God's Son (christological method, life, death, resurrection, ascension and session of Jesus, and how Jesus relates to God's identity), the gospel of salvation (redemptive history, order of salvation, images of salvation, scope and security), the promise and power of the gospel—the Holy Spirit (the breath of the gospel, person, and work), and the gospel and humanity (sons and daughters, image of God, what humanity is, the problem and the odyssey of theodicy), and Bird finishes with the community of the gospelized (evangelical church, images of church, shape and marks and governance of the church, and the emblems of the gospel in baptism and the Lord's Supper). Bird's facility in biblical studies as well in theology makes his theology a fresh development in the evangelical theological tradition.

The framing of theology by creed or by topic is inadequate to biblical revelation. The Bible's own framing of theology is not to give a systematics or a list of what to believe but instead is an ongoing narrative of development. As a Bible guy, I'd urge systematicians to rethink the frame and consider a more narrative one.

WHAT DOES IT MEAN THAT GOD SPOKE AS GOD DID?

I speak here for those on the Bible side of the ledger. We read systematics and sometimes feel as if we are in a foreign land listening to

---

[9]N. T. Wright, *What Saint Paul Really Said: Was Paul of Tarsus the Real Founder of Christianity?* (Grand Rapids, MI: Eerdmans, 1997); Scot McKnight, *The King Jesus Gospel: The Original Good News Revisited*, 2nd ed. (Grand Rapids, MI: Zondervan, 2015). One could cite dozens of works by Wright.

acquaintances speaking in a foreign language about what we both believe. At times, of course, this is because of the erudition of the scholars—only specialists can absorb Lewis Ayres's *Nicaea and Its Legacy* and make sense of every paragraph—but also at times this is because of the third, fourth, and fifth levels of conversation, in which so-and-so said one thing, and so-and-so added to it, and then so-and-so revised it, and now we know that revision needed some fine-tuning by a book others were ignoring . . . and so on, until one enters the room and wonders what's being talked about. (I know, I know, systematicians feel this way about erudite discussions of Greek tenses and exegetical nuances. We all at times resort to Mona Lisa smiles.) Say it any way you want, but the Bible people will admit they haven't kept up with theological developments in systematics. Say it again, and you will see one more time that we live in different homes on the same street and have been separated from the other for so long that we don't know a new discourse has formed.

Why say this? Too many systematicians have ignored the Bible's own way of presenting theology. The Bible is a long, drawn-out narrative of sorts, and without that narrative even those well-studied lines by Paul in Romans 3:21-26 don't seem to fit into the theological location they're given in some systematic textbooks and monographs. When we frame of theology in terms of the three articles, we think in their terms—Father, Son, and Spirit (and church and forgiveness and eternal life). When we frame theology by topics, we are basically thinking in terms of soteriology, and everything is extruded through soteriology. If the main topics are God, humanity, Christ, sin and salvation, ecclesiology, and eschatology (where's pneumatology?)— we are thinking in terms of (nearly always) personal salvation. Fine and good, except in thinking like either of these two approaches we are not always thinking in the Bible's own terms, and we Bible people ask, Which has the greater weight—the Bible or the framing of some (not all!) topics into a coherent system reshaped by both philosophy and the history of theological discourse? We on the Bible side of the ledger answer that question with, "The B-I-B-L-E!"

In stating above that the Bible is a narrative or a story, I need to add with emphasis that the various books of the Bible are in various genres, and within books there are a variety of genres as well as rhetorics. Perhaps because of the diverse voices of the Bible, we have learned to settle with some common denominator, or some agreed-on theological statements, and then we move on. Should we surrender the Bible's own approach to the topics? No. Is moving on perhaps part of the problem? Yes. That is, are we so used to the topics that it would take a generation of rethinking to provide a new frame for theology? Yes.

D. A. Carson, speaking for many on the Bible side, has weighed in at precisely this point a number of times in a lengthy career, and here I cite from his entry on "Systematic Theology and Biblical Theology."[10]

> As its name suggests, systematic theology attempts to organize, to systematize, theological reflection. When the primary authoritative source for that theological synthesis and reflection is the Bible, systematic theology attempts to organize what the Bible says according to some system. The traditional tenfold division of topics is certainly not the only possibility. But even to choose topics, to hierarchialize them, is to impose a structure not transparently given in Scripture itself. In any case, such theological reflection inevitably emerges out of one epistemology or another out of a particular cultural consciousness, and such matters will become correspondingly more influential in the system to the degree that the theologian is unaware of them or holds, naively, that they have little or no influence.[11]

---

[10]D. A. Carson, "Systematic Theology and Biblical Theology," in *New Dictionary of Biblical Theology*, ed. T. Desmond Alexander and Brian S. Rosner (Downers Grove, IL: InterVarsity Press, 2000), 89-104.

[11]Carson, "Systematic Theology," 101.

I agree. He continues,

> There are deeper issues. The Bible speaks in highly diverse lit-
> erary genres that play upon our hearts and minds in a great
> variety of speech acts. To encapsulate this diversity and power
> within the form of a systematic theology is to demand too much
> of the discipline. But the systematic theologian can mitigate the
> most obvious dangers by wide reading in the literature of exe-
> gesis and by delving deeply into biblical theology as a mediating
> discipline. The systematician must recognize, further, the in-
> herent limitations of systematic theology. For all its strengths,
> there are many things it cannot do. It can analyse a lament within
> the biblical corpus, but it cannot evoke a heart-felt lament in
> the way a lament itself can. It may expound the meaning of some
> parables, but it cannot explode the reader's worldview in the
> way the most striking of the narrative parables can.[12]

I agree with the first but have no idea why he thinks a systematic
theology "cannot" do some of these things. It surely can, if it chooses
to. Perhaps his *cannot* means "does not normally do." Then he points
to the problem that Bible folks typically have with systematicians:
"Nevertheless, once a particular systematic theology has been deeply
absorbed, precisely because it is worldview forming it is likely to exercise significant influence on the disciplines that nurture it: exegesis,
biblical theology, historical theology. The hermeneutical circle is
joined, but not vicious." He adds, "What is transparently clear about
all such systematic theology, however, is that its organizing principles
do not encourage the exploration of the Bible's plot line, except inci-
dentally. The categories of systematic theology are logical and hierarchical, not temporal."[13] Once again, agreed. Here is his own
summary comparison of biblical theology and systematic theology:

---

[12]Carson, "Systematic Theology," 101-2.
[13]Carson, "Systematic Theology," 102.

Systematic theology seeks to rearticulate what the Bible says in self-conscious engagement with (including confrontation with) the culture; biblical theology, though it cannot escape cultural influences, aims to be first and foremost inductive and descriptive, earning its normative power by the credibility of its results. Thus systematic theology tends to be a little further removed from the biblical text than does biblical theology, but a little closer to cultural engagement. Biblical theology tends to seek out the rationality and communicative genius of each literary genre; systematic theology tends to integrate the diverse rationalities in its pursuit of a large-scale, worldview-forming synthesis. In this sense, systematic theology tends to be a culminating discipline; biblical theology, though it is a worthy end in itself, tends to be a bridge discipline.[14]

More or less, that is a common biblical scholar's understanding of the differences. Many, however, would never cede to systematics that biblical theology is but a bridge discipline. Many, in fact, would want to call the systematicians back across the bridge and then narrow the lanes and slow down the traffic.[15]

As a Bible professor, I myself ask this question often when I'm done reading systematic studies: Where's Israel? Where's Abraham (other than someone who was cited by Paul in Galatians and Romans)? Where are David and Solomon and the issue of kings? What about Miriam, Deborah, Esther, and Huldah? Where are the prophets, other than folks who put forth theological statements represented in the New Testament? Where, in fact, is history as the stage on which God plays out redemption for the world? Where's the exodus? The exile? The land? The city? What is the plot? Put more bluntly, where is the plot? Where is Jesus and the kingdom? In my estimation, no matter

---

[14]Carson, "Systematic Theology," 103.
[15]The irony is that I have always thought Carson himself is too influenced by his Calvinism.

how noble the thoughts and articulations, the three-article frame has *no plot whatsoever,* while the topic frame has a *personal salvation* plot. I do not dispute the clarifications that both of these frames have brought for the church. Not at all. I question the *adequacy* of the frames, and I press theologians to ponder a narrative frame for doing systematics. I don't tire of saying this: *God did not reveal a systematics but instead spoke into history over time and in a diversity of ways through a myriad of persons and a myriad of locations and contexts.* The fancy term here is *exigencies. What does how God speaks to us in the Bible tell us about doing theology?* The three-article and the topic frames squelch too much by their frame, and there is a way, I believe, for Christian theology to become more adequate in frame without denying the insights of the three-article and topic frames.

One might at this point apologize to theologians who, while framing a three-article or topics frame, have worked narratively within each topic to form the substance of their theology. This, at least, is attempted in important ways by some, and I see not enough of this in Katherine Sonderegger, some glimpses in Robert Jenson, and more than glimpses in Michael Bird. These glimpses must be appreciated, if at the same time this Bible guy wonders what theology might look like if it were done in an even more narrative frame.

A NARRATIVE FRAME FOR THEOLOGY

I begin with some recent definitions of narrative theology, taking that expression as a general indicator of what we need. Joel Green puts it this way:[16]

> "Narrative theology" refers to a constellation of approaches to the theological task typically joined by their (1) antipathy toward forms of theology concerned with the systematic

---

[16]J. B. Green, "Narrative Theology," in *Dictionary for Theological Interpretation of the Bible,* ed. Kevin J. Vanhoozer (Grand Rapids, MI: Baker Academic, 2005), 531-33.

organization of propositions and grounded in ahistorical principles, and (2) attempt to discern an overall aim and ongoing plot in the ways of God as these are revealed in Scripture and continue to express themselves in history.[17]

His first point rules off the table the framing of theology by the three articles or topics. Rather than framing theology by propositions, narrative theologians seek to "discern an overall aim and ongoing plot in the ways of God as these are revealed in Scripture and continue to express themselves in history." Green further observes that the Bible is filled with narratives, not least Genesis through Esther! That is, approximately 495 of almost 1,000 pages in John Goldingay's *The First Testament* translation are narrative. The first five books of the second testament, too, are narratives. That is, approximately 400 of 680 pages of my Greek New Testament. God is known through events and contexts. Green again:

> The importance of narrative theology is underscored by the recognition that narrative is central to identity formation; indeed, recent work in neurobiology emphasizes the capacity for and drive toward making *storied sense* of our experienced world as a distinguishing characteristic of the human family. We typically explain our behaviors through the historical narratives by which we collaborate to create a sense of ourselves as persons and as a people. The story we embrace serves as an interpretative scheme that is at once *conceptual* (a way of seeing things), *conative* (a set of beliefs and values to which a group and its members are deeply attached), and *action-guiding* (we seek to live according to its terms).[18]

One must at least question the adequacy of the three-article or topic frames for humans, who make sense of life through *stories*. What

---

[17]Green, "Narrative Theology," 531.
[18]Green, "Narrative Theology," 532.

Green says here represents well the narrative frame that is a current challenge to systematics as we know it.

BUT WHICH NARRATIVE?

It's quite simple to lay down the observation that systematic theology falls short because it is not framed by narrative. The Bible is comprehended by a series of books—from Genesis to Malachi, from Matthew to Revelation—that never stop to put it all into a single document. While many think Paul's letter to the Romans, abbreviated perhaps in an earlier form in Galatians, is just that book, that's wrong for more than a few reasons—including that Romans is itself a highly contingent letter to a specific church for a specific time about specific issues, and that it remains but one apostle's theological summary, while there are other apostolic summaries in 1 Peter and 1 John and James.[19] Let's also add that, after all, Jesus is the Lord, and his teachings on the kingdom (Synoptic Gospels) and eternal life (John) are yet another kind of theology. So, to take Romans as the fundamental systematic of the Bible is wrong even for the New Testament.[20] I'll drop the point here that most topic frames of systematics are obviously theologies developed out of Romans with very little regard for kingdom, eternal life, or the priesthood themes of Hebrews. This is the greatest weaknesses of the topic frames as well as the creedal frames—and Tom Wright has himself pushed back against the frame of the creeds for their lack of attention to kingdom theology.[21] New Testament specialists push back even harder when systematicians brush this criticism to the side or think the creed after all is kingdom theology.

---

[19] Scot McKnight, *Reading Romans Backwards: A Gospel of Peace in the Midst of Empire* (Waco, TX: Baylor University Press, 2019).

[20] John Calvin's *Institutes* are formed on top of Romans, as many have noted. E.g., Sarah Coakley, *God, Sexuality, and the Self: An Essay "On the Trinity"* (Cambridge: Cambridge University Press, 2013), 39.

[21] N. T. Wright, *How God Became King: The Forgotten Story of the Gospels* (New York: HarperOne, 2012).

So, what then about narrative? A narrative is made of characters and events in a plot line, as well as crucial ideas and interpretive moves made by the narrator, and at least some tension of how to get from beginning to end. One could list the most significant characters: Adam and his oft-neglected partner, Eve; Abram-become-Abraham and his oft-neglected partner, Sarai-become-Sarah; the patriarchs (Isaac, Jacob, Joseph); Moses; Aaron; Joshua and the crazy uncle judges; Samuel; Saul; David; Solomon and the kings of the northern and southern kingdoms; the prophets (Isaiah to Malachi); Jesus and his oft-neglected mother, Mary; the apostles (especially Peter and Paul); and a few other names tossed in (Barnabas, Priscilla and Aquila, Phoebe, Lydia, and others). Then major events: creation, fall, covenant formation with Abram, the children of Israel in Egypt and their liberation under Moses, the giving of the law, entering the land, conquering the land, the demand for a king, ups and downs of obedience and disobedience, exile, return, the Messiah's arrival, the death and burial and resurrection and ascension of Jesus, the gift of the Spirit, the mission of the church.

The plot line moves from creation to kingdom come. Tensions appear for each event and set up tensions for later events. Add to these crucial ideas such as image of God, sin, covenant, kingdom, salvation, law, kingship, prophetic word, exile, return, discipleship, justice, love, holiness, temple, sacrifice, Messiah, Spirit, apostleship, and relation to ruling powers. Throw into the mix, in a way that captures all of it, the story of Israel and the story of the church. On top of these are moments when interpretive moves are made: expelling Adam and Eve from Eden, the zaniness of attempting to build a tower in Babel to God's heights, the promise of a people through covenant formation, the giving of a land in which to dwell with God in faithfulness, law as covenant life, exile as discipline for disobedience, return as a sign of God's covenant faithfulness, the prophets denouncing injustices with promise of blessing for faithfulness, the expectation of a messianic king who will usher in God's kingdom for ever and ever, the blessing of the Spirit on a people to engage in universal mission, the longing and expectation of a universal revival of all to worship the one true God and his Son through the Spirit— and there are others, but these are enough to make one thing clear: *yes, there is a narrative to be sorted out.*

But this only leads to a bigger problem: if one can state unequivocally that systematics in the topic frame are one-sidedly and even narrowly dependent on Romans to the neglect of Jesus' own teachings (!), one can argue that there is also no one narrative. There is more than one way to coordinate these characters, events, and ideas in a meaning-shaping narrative. Compare 1–2 Kings with 1–2 Chronicles, and one finds differing takes on largely the same people and events, and then read Nehemiah 9–10 to see a summary statement of something like those longer narratives but not the same, and then read Acts 7's account of those people and events. Within the Bible, then, there is not one narrative. When Jewish historian Josephus chose to put it all into a narrative—*Antiquities of the Jews*—he took these biblical books and recast them into his own kind of narrative. What then about the history-of-Israel approach to reading the Old Testament? Whose critical sifting tells the story the best? The most accurately? But these examples are about Israel's history. What about the whole Bible? What's the narrative?

One example makes this clear. The most common narrative of the Bible, one I have often used in teaching, is the four-chapter narrative composed of creation, fall, redemption, and consummation. However useful this narrative might be, and I believe I first learned this narrative reading Geerhardus Vos as a college student, I'm not so sure anyone in the Bible actually uses this narrative other than Paul in Romans. Even there it is a bowdlerized version of a complex narrative that is found in Romans 5 but largely neglects the permutations of that narrative in Romans 9–11. What convinced me that this narrative is not the Bible's narrative but one reductionistic narrative in the Bible is that, if one begins with Jesus and asks which narrative he was using, the answer is *kingdom*. But that four-chapter narrative does not create the need for a kingdom, unless one begins to fidget and fudge (as some have done of late by pretending covenant and kingdom are the same, or that salvation/justification and kingdom are the same). Rather, Jesus was more in tune with 1 Samuel 8's lame request for a king than with redemption in covenant terms. This may sound shocking to some, but Jesus did not think with the term *covenant* but with the term *kingdom*, so what is needed to comprehend Jesus' narrative is the longing for the kingdom of God.

One example from a systematician: When Robert Jenson gets to his chapter on Jesus, he chooses a theology of Word à la Rudolf Bultmann, which is a Lutheran perception of faith filtered both through Paul and John. His (all too brief) sketch of kingdom evokes Günther Bornkamm's eschatological tenor (Jesus is himself the immanence of the kingdom) but does not satisfy modern biblical scholarship.[22] What Jenson does not do is study kingdom in its narrative plot in the Bible—and most who have theologized about kingdom have done the same.

Where in the common creation, fall, redemption, and consummation is there any noticeable presence of structural and systemic evil? Of a God who invades the world to liberate humans from bondage? Of a kingdom marked by justice and peace so penetratingly that the end shapes the narrative such that we must begin all over again and tell a different story? This is precisely what liberation theologians such as Elsa Támez have done to great effect. A common

---

[22]Jenson, *Systematic Theology*, 1:165-78. Here is his summary statement: "Jesus the Christ, in his full historical reality of birth, life, death, and resurrection, is the Word of God in that he is the identity of the future opened by the Word of God. He is the Word of God in that he is the narrative content of the proclamation that, because it poses eschatological possibility, is the Word of God. He is the Word of God because he is the narrative content of the word-event that is the Word of God" (1:171).

response (by the creation-fall-redemption-consummation propo-
nents) is that such a narrative is biased both in intention and exe-
cution, and the response by someone like Támez is: "Indeed, so it is.
So is yours!" What the liberationist narrative unmasks is the location
of other narratives that determine what to look for in the Bible and
therefore determine what is found. "If we accept," she says, "that sin
has to do with social reality, justification also has to be understood
within the same horizon."[23]

That conclusion leads to an entirely reshaped narrative. When sin
gains its biblical proportions, so too does justification. Reconciliation
is no longer just a human with their God but also humans with
humans, and the individualistic frame of modernity is challenged, if
not defeated. The study of the Jewish roots of justification in the
Hebrew *tsedeq/tsedeqah* reveals, too, that righteousness or rightness
cannot be limited to the personal soul and the personal God but must
extend to God's will for all of creation, and that justification becomes
God making things right for all of creation. Justification, Támez contends, entails affirmation of the life of each person, and this can only
mean that justification is a force of liberation for the poor. Why?
Because of texts such as Romans 4:25, where justification is connected to resurrection and thus to new creation. Suddenly, we learn
to see justification connected to liberation from Egypt, new life in the
new land, return from exile, and hope for a world marked by justice.
History, too, becomes a subject of discussion as now the justified and
liberated are launched into a new project of working for justice in the
world by dismantling oppressions.

Narrative approaches to Scripture, like systematics, tend to think
there is *one* narrative that puts the whole Bible together, and one can
accumulate the major names and events and ideas and so construct
a narrative of some sort (this is what many Old Testament history

---

[23]Elsa Támez, *The Amnesty of Grace: Justification by Faith from a Latin American Perspective,*
trans. Sharon H. Ringe (Nashville: Abingdon, 1991), 21.

classes do). Such a narrative is the constructor's and not one held by any single author of the Bible. Another admission may be even more important: *Christian narrative theologians construct a narrative on the basis of the revelation of God in Christ.* One has learned to be suspect of narratives that think they are starting at Genesis 1 and moving forward until . . . suddenly the pieces all fitting together . . . there is Christ! A theologian especially sensitive to narrative, Jenson, expresses this very point: "A story is constituted by the outcome of the narrated events."[24] That statement by itself articulates a narrative theology in its fullness, though one must study the outcome carefully to know how the narrative has been constituted. Some pages later he expands on that simple (and clear) articulation:

> The future that opens a narratable history shapes that history, and after the fact this shaping may sometimes be discerned. Vice versa, what can be seen to shape a plotted history must, if the discernment is true, in some future occur within that history. Or, at least, so the church from the first understood history: the fathers' practice of "spiritual" exegesis was intended to trace the one history told by Scripture as in each specious present plotted by its coming fulfillment. They understood the narrated events as in themselves prophecy, precisely insofar as they could be construed as a sequence plotted by its final future. Nor was such reading understood as an imposition of meaning on the "literal" meaning; the fathers claimed to see the narrative's "allegory" of its own fulfillment not above or beyond the narrated facts but *in* them.[25]

In spite of the denseness of prose about futurity, I think he's got this right: the narrative's futurity, once it happens, both gives the narrative its dramatic coherence and sheds light on how to read that narrative. What is latent becomes obvious only after the future is clear. To jump

---

[24]Jenson, *Systematic Theology*, 1:66.
[25]Jenson, *Systematic Theology*, 1:81-82.

lanes briefly into another conversation, this is not far from what the apocalyptic Paul scholars are saying, though I believe they press this point in ways that go well beyond what Jenson is saying. He clearly states the Old Testament narrative has futurity written into it, while the apocalyptic scholars tend to diminish that futurity and see it all apocalyptic (i.e., revealed) in a shatteringly new way in Jesus.[26] Jenson anchors this futurity in creation itself in his seventh point about God's creation: "The world God creates is not a thing, a 'cosmos,' but is rather a history."[27]

There is, I am arguing, no single narrative that puts the whole Bible together other than using all the names, all the events, all the ideas, and all the interpretive moves, so I want here to put one of the major narratives into shape, one that finds its future in the kingdom hermeneutic of Jesus. Instead of the four-chapter frame I propose here (to comprehend Jesus), here is a three-chapter frame of theocracy, monarchy, and christocracy (God rules, a king rules, Christ the king rules).

Theocracy

1. God is Creator God, God is covenant-maker God. (Gen 1–2)

2. Humans are charged to be kings and priests in the cosmic temple. (Gen 2)

3. Humans usurp God's role and are driven from Eden. (Gen 3)

---

[26]The apocalyptic scholar from whom I have learned the most on this is Douglas Campbell. I mention here only Campbell, *The Quest for Paul's Gospel* (London: T&T Clark, 2005); Campbell, *The Deliverance of God: An Apocalyptic Rereading of Justification in Paul* (Grand Rapids, MI: Eerdmans, 2013); Campbell, "Apocalyptic Epistemology: The Sine Qua Non of Valid Pauline Interpretation," in *Paul and the Apocalyptic Imagination*, ed. Ben C. Blackwell, John K. Goodrich, and Jason Maston (Minneapolis: Fortress, 2016), 65-85; Campbell, *Pauline Dogmatics: The Triumph of God's Love* (Grand Rapids, MI: Eerdmans, 2020). The apocalyptic Paul scholars have been criticized especially in N. T. Wright, *Pauline Perspectives: Essays on Paul, 1978–2013* (Minneapolis: Fortress, 2013); Wright, *The Paul Debate: Critical Questions for Understanding the Apostle* (Waco, TX: Baylor University Press, 2015). His most forceful attempt to create an alternative historiography is Wright, *History and Eschatology: Jesus and the Promise of Natural Theology* (Waco, TX: Baylor University Press, 2019).
[27]Jenson, *Systematic Theology*, 2:14. Jenson believes, too, that in creating God makes room or accommodates creation to share in the divine life of the Trinity, all of which is connected to this theory of time and distention—which I should not attempt to summarize here (even if I could). "God takes time in his time for us" (2:35).

4. Humans flounder in usurpation. (Gen 4–11, especially Babel)

5. Humans are brought into shape through God's covenant election of Abraham, and Israel is governed by the Torah through Moses. (Gen 12 through Deuteronomy)

6. The divine plan was for God to rule through one people—Israel. (Joshua, Judges, Historical Books)

Monarchy

7. There is, upon request, a divine permission to have a king (1 Sam 8), and God took a monarchy and made it his own: God will rule through one people (Israel) represented by one king (David and successors; 2 Sam 7).

8. The monarchy failed in spite of divine disciplines: the Northern Kingdom is exiled to Assyria, the Southern Kingdom to Babylon and then Persia and Rome. (Prophets)

Christocracy

9. Divine rule is reinstated in Christ: God rules through one people (Israel) but himself rules through his one and only Son, King Jesus, and King Jesus is the Lord of both Jews and Gentiles. (Gospels)

10. The christocracy therefore extends God's rule through Israel, under King Jesus, to the world of Gentiles through the church. The church does not replace Israel; the church expands Israel. That is, Israel expanded is the church. (Acts, Pauline letters; see esp. Rom 11:17-24)

11. Christocracy entails generations of mission to expand Israel/church into the whole world. (church history)

12. Christocracy is consummated in the new heavens and the new earth in a new Jerusalem, where God will rule through the Lamb, who is the new temple. This is the kingdom of God. (Rev 20–22)

This narrative is not found in any systematic theology, but it can feasibly be said to be the narrative at work in Jesus and the mission of the church, and if that is approximately the case, systematic theology is formed apart from Jesus' own narrative.

Again, this is a narrative that (for me at least) best explains the narrative Jesus was using, but it does not explain the narrative framework at work for the apostles John, Paul, Peter, or James, and it does not get us into the narrative at work behind the book of Hebrews. There is some overlap in my narrative above with the book of Revelation, but Revelation has its own narrative, and it, too, needs to be seen for what it is. If one wants a narrative whose future is Paul's, then one has to construct a narrative with Adam and Abraham and Moses gaining the strongest voices, events, and ideas. But it's not necessary to create a series of narratives, because there is, ironically, no single narratival hermeneutic (say, the creation-fall-redemption-consummation narrative) that unites the whole Bible, though there are narratives that cohere with what is going on in the Bible. Each of the various narratives of all the authors of the Bible is operating with the basic characters, events, and ideas, but each also brings fresh interpretive moves to bring the narrative up to date for the author's own audience. Complicating the narrative frame is that the narrative grows over time. We get new characters, fresh events that force us to reframe our old narratives, and we get new ideas (kingdom is mostly new to Jesus, justification is mostly new to Paul, the sacrificial priesthood themes of Hebrews take Leviticus to a new level, eternal life is not found in that form anywhere until John) and therefore new interpretive moves. The narrative is kaleidoscopic: the same pieces are in the tube, but one's angle and one's light refracts a different vision.

This is why both the three-article and the topics frame fall short. They aren't big enough or wide enough or deep enough to handle all the characters, events, ideas, and interpretive moves found in the Bible itself. Some of them don't even try, and because they don't try there is so much left out. There is stuff that seems not to matter to some systematicians and thus stuff that can be ignored, such as Jephthah or Ananias and Sapphira. But we are the ones who lose when our systems bracket out stuff that doesn't fit. Eugene Peterson, a Bible reader if ever there was one, says it well:

> The most frequent way we have of getting rid of the puzzling or unpleasant difficulties in the Bible is to systematize it, organizing it according to some scheme or other that summarizes "what the Bible teaches." If we know what the Bible teaches, we don't have to read it anymore, don't have to enter the story and immerse ourselves in the odd and unflattering and uncongenial way in which this story develops, including so many people and circumstances that have nothing to do, we think, with us.[28]

Only a narrative frame will take us beyond the three-article and topics frame in a way that says whatever is there fits where it belongs, and that omitting it—like refusing to tell the story of some crazy uncle or a dysfunctional cousin—will affect the story and our theology.

NARRATIVE MEANS PROGRESS IS THE PARADIGM

I was standing on a platform in Seattle speaking about this wiki-story approach when it dawned on me in front of everyone that anyone who adheres to a narrative frame for the Bible embraces an expansive model. I have long been bothered by the holy war passages in the First Testament. What bothers me more is that some people in our churches use them to justify nuclear proliferation and nothing less than seemingly sadistic deaths in war. When I read these passages, I sense they are not in sync with the vision of Jesus in the Gospels or the apostles. The paradigm of Jesus for interacting with enemies is to love them, to die for them, to work to be reconciled with them, and to help them

---

[28]Eugene Peterson, *Eat This Book: A Conversation in the Art of Spiritual Reading* (Grand Rapids, MI: Baker, 2006), 66.

become reconciled with God. Behind the apostle Paul's own Christoform theology, as seen in Philippians 2:6-11, is nothing less than a cruciform approach to interpersonal relations. What does Jesus and what do the apostles say about the holy war texts in Israel's story?

There are really only two options: either we keep the holy war texts as viable teachings or we think there is some level of progress in the Bible such that Jesus' vision annuls the holy war texts. William Webb and Gordon Oeste, in their new book *Bloody, Brutal, and Barbaric?*, propose the following seven implications of what happens to holy war texts once they sit down at dinner with Jesus:

1. The cross marks a unique change or advancement in the canonical story line that stops the recurring ethical damage from literal holy war ever happening again (not unlike the end of literal animal sacrifice). It does so by moving holy war (fighting between human armies) from the literal to the spiritual/ metaphorical domain.

2. The extreme cruelty and injustice experienced by Jesus in his warlike crucifixion by Roman soldiers (the horizon of shared ancient-world atrocities) makes him uniquely qualified to hear, judge, and untangle the ethical mess of those who experienced embedded (in)justice in ancient biblical holy war.

3. The cross-all-nations extension of the death of Jesus and his gospel should make us at least open to, if not inclined to, seeing the final eschatological battle in a metaphorical (not literal) light.

4. The portrait of a suffering and crying God both in the cross of Jesus and in the holy war texts takes us deep into the mystery of divine love and vulnerability. While this does not directly fix the ethical problem, it surely helps us realize where God is in all this suffering. It is hard to remain angry at someone who suffers with us in a suffering world.

5. The torn temple curtain at the death of Jesus and emerging new-temple ideas completely reconfigure the temple-land-nation ideology of the Old Testament and ancient world. Any land-tied, nation-based literal warfare becomes obsolete and nonsensical for Jesus' followers, who worship in a new, people-based temple.

6. The coming of the Spirit confirms new-temple theology but also affords the opportunity for taking the ethics of biblical warfare (its laws) with its incremental redemptive movement to new levels of fulfillment well beyond Hague and Geneva. On a personal level we are called to be less retaliatory (no longer punch for punch) and more giving (go the extra mile).

7. Jesus' death and empty tomb carry the redemptive story line forward to the point of final justice. The unfolding implications of crucifixion, resurrection, and ascension lie deep within the spiritual substrata of what it takes to make the next thing happen. The first-advent Jesus events create the theological impetus that makes it possible for the story line to move forward toward a much-awaited moment in the eschaton—the ultimate resolution of all past injustices with the coming of the final and complete justice that Jesus brings to the new heavens and new earth.[29]

Not all want to dance with Webb and Oeste; some will prefer the more theological interpretive grid offered by Greg Boyd.[30] But what few will countenance is flat-footed affirmation of the holy war texts, which means that most have learned to dance on a new dance floor with Jesus, and that means some kind of expansive narrative frame for doing theology *within the Bible itself.*

---

[29]William J. Webb and Gordon K. Oeste, *Bloody, Brutal, and Barbaric? Wrestling with Troubling War Texts* (Downers Grove, IL: IVP Academic, 2019), 333-34.
[30]Gregory A. Boyd, *The Crucifixion of the Warrior God* (Minneapolis: Fortress, 2017).

Holy war texts are of course an easier category to address in this instance than some others, but it's not so easy to slip the hook as one might think. All Christians read the Bible in an expansive way because all affirm that Jesus is the long-awaited Messiah and that the law was dealt some serious checks in Mark 7:19; Acts 10; Romans 7 or Romans 9–11; Galatians 3; and also in Hebrews. Progress is the name once one embraces a narrative frame.

NARRATIVE MEANS ECCLESIOLOGY IS CENTRAL

In the three-article frame of the creed there are four, not three, instances of "We believe": the Father, the Son, and the Spirit, but there is also tucked into that third article, "We believe in one holy, catholic, and apostolic church." This stands out as a fourth element of the creed that is diminished in many of the topic frames of theology. Depending on who's doing the theology, the church can be diminished as well in three-article frames. I see it very little in Sarah Coakley's systematic theology. Her work is not yet complete, so time will tell whether she pulls church into the heart of her trinitarian theology.

The narrative frame, however, emphasizes the church. It is boilerplate to criticize systematics for their emphasis on individual and personal salvation, especially in the Reformation wing of the church, but boilerplate often arises because something is true. When the topics frame suspends ecclesiology until a later topic, it runs the risk of diminishing ecclesiology until one gets there, and the same at times occurs in the three-article frame. The fact is that the Old Testament simply isn't telling the story of personal salvation very often. What, then, is in view? Yes, salvation does appear, but it is almost entirely *about corporate or group redemption*. Yes, the Bible is about salvation, but it is about salvation of the people of God for the purpose of accomplishing the mission of God in the world. Reading the Bible from Genesis to Malachi is to encounter one story after another about Israel and about the kings and prophets of Israel. It is about God's ways with the people of Israel. We make a colossal mistake if we then enter the New Testament and begin to think entirely in terms of individual redemption, though personal healing (often called salvation in the Gospels) and personal conversion to Jesus is given lots of attention. Rather, the core of Paul's and Peter's and John's writings is the church, the people of God in Christ. A narrative frame for theology cannot but bring the people of God to the forefront of the story, because that's what the Bible is about. Read Acts, and one encounters there the story of the growth especially of the Pauline churches from Jerusalem to Rome.

What puts the Bible together is that it is a story of Israel leading to the story of Jesus, the apostles, and the church. What puts the Bible together, then, is that it is the church's story about Jesus. What shocks the narrative theologian of the Bible is the minimization of church in the three-article frame and the postponement of ecclesiology until a later topic in the topics frame. The Bible's central theology is a narrative about God's ways with a people (Israel, church). The Bible's theology is a story, and without that story framing theology, we lose the centrality of the Bible's own frame.

CONCLUSION

Frames matter immensely to what happens with theology, and I'm persuaded that the history of Christian theology has been locked down in utter brilliance with its three-article and topics frames and is in need of a reframing—one that takes into consideration the narrative of the Bible. I am also convinced that ethics should be not be relegated to a late chapter in the topics frame. Theology that is not lived is not theology, and I turn to that in the next chapter, but in doing so I want to put together our entire method that has so far been proposed. Theology is multidisciplinary, exegetical, historical, narratival, and—all of it—meant to be embodied in such a way that *life is the theology*.

THEOLOGY NEEDS TO BE LIVED THEOLOGY

IT IS NOT AN OVERSTATEMENT TO SAY one will be judged not by one's theology but by one's life. Every theologian now raises a hand to remind the one saying such a thing that it may be worse than an overstatement. *What* one believes matters. Yes, I want to start with that, and these two books—Boersma's and mine—stand on that. But believing the right things is not enough. Living what we believe matters, and this final chapter contends that a theology that is not a lived theology falls short. Ethics is sometimes one of the topics in theology in the topics frame. The three-article frame, one must observe, has next to nothing about ethics. One could infer ethical corollaries from one or two of the separate lines in the creed, as in "he will come to judge the living and the dead" and "forgiveness of sins." Stretch it as one will, that frame lacks ethics at the heart of what we believe. Some may then push back to say, "Well, the creed after all is about what we *believe* and not about how we *live*" ... and the response is even more obvious: living is what believing is all about. Theology, Adam Neder has recently reminded us, is for life.[1]

It is not just the three-article frame that neglects ethics but also the topics frame. Most tend to submerge ethics into soteriology, and thus into sanctification, which (I am quick to add) is an entirely reasonable place for ethics. Karl Barth makes ethics a topic and in his usual manner integrates the entirety of his theology into it. Barth stood alongside Dietrich Bonhoeffer while the latter was alive and watched the young man's theology come into view, and what Bonhoeffer was doing was nothing less than a theological ethics. We don't know what would have become of Bonhoeffer's theology had he lived a normal span. One has to wonder—or I know I have to—whether the difference here is between one whose theology permeated all of his ethics so much that his ethics was his theology (Bonhoeffer) and one whose ethics was an outworking of his theology (Barth). Robert Jenson grabs my attention when he says ethics is part of ecclesiology: "Discussion of specifically Christian life belongs to the doctrine of the church, not in a separate department of its own."[2] The Christian is the one through whom the church expresses itself; the church is where the Christian is truly Christian. What follows, I hope, puts that statement into reality as I seek to show that systematic theology is insufficiently framed by lived theology and that lived theology can help us all frame theology in a more biblical manner.

THE BIBLE'S ANGLE ON THEOLOGY

Theology abstracted from ethics or from lived theology is not biblical theology. Ancient Israel's theology was as integrated into ethics as its ethics was integrated into its theology. The two are inseparable, and it is only some version of cognitive behaviorism or mind over matter

---

[1]Adam Neder, *Theology as a Way of Life: On Teaching and Learning the Christian Life* (Grand Rapids, MI: Baker Academic, 2019).
[2]Robert W. Jenson, *Systematic Theology* (New York: Oxford University Press, 1997), 2:289.

that permits the separation. It is one of the oldest theological mistakes to divorce how we live from what we believe. The covenant God made with Abram/Abraham, the covenant God made with Moses, the covenant God made with David, the new covenant God promised through Jeremiah and Ezekiel—that multiformed covenant was as much an ethics as it was a theology. Torah is not theoretical morality but lived theology, a life enflamed by knowing God. Yes, at times it moves from theology to ethics, as in God saying that because I am holy, you (Israel) are to be holy. But it's a simplistic error to think the two can be separated.

Take, for instance, James 2:14-19:

> What good is it, my brothers and sisters, if you say you have faith but do not have works? Can faith save you? If a brother or sister is naked and lacks daily food, and one of you says to them, "Go in peace; keep warm and eat your fill," and yet you do not supply their bodily needs, what is the good of that? So faith by itself, if it has no works, is dead.
>
> But someone will say, "You have faith and I have works." Show me your faith apart from your works, and I by my works will show you my faith. You believe that God is one; you do well. Even the demons believe—and shudder.

James, for one, can't abide a theology that is not lived. "Faith by itself," he says, is "dead." One is an inch from James if one uses the word *theology* instead of the word *faith* here, and thus James would be saying that theology by itself is dead if it is not lived.

Take Paul's words to Timothy too. In a passage that gets more attention for its use of the term *inspiration* than for its fundamental direction, we read this:

> But as for you, continue in what you have learned and firmly believed, knowing from whom you learned it, and how from childhood you have known the sacred writings that are able to

instruct you for salvation through faith in Christ Jesus. All scripture is inspired by God and is useful for teaching, for reproof, for correction, and for training in righteousness, so that everyone who belongs to God may be proficient, equipped for every good work. (2 Tim 3:14-17)

Timothy came to faith through his mother and grandmother (and Paul here is ignoring his own impact on the young man). In that family he learned the art of sacred Scripture that has a goal in mind: "so that everyone who belongs to God may be proficient," which means "equipped for every good work." Scripture promotes theology in a direction: life. A theology that doesn't get to that life is not what God has in mind, and it's an incomplete theology.

The most significant passage in the Bible about the Bible is not, however, those two poignant New Testament passages that have given to us words such as *inspiration* (2 Tim 3:14-17; 2 Pet 1:20-21). Rather, it is Psalm 119, and it can be read as the Bible's view of the Bible. It uses eight different terms for what we call the Bible: *Torah* or *law* or *instruction* (25×), *word* (24×), *rulings* and *covenant* (23×), *commands* (22×), *statutes* and *charges* (21×), and *sayings* (19×). Every bit of this very long psalm inculcates a knowing that is a doing, a doing that emerges from knowing, and a doing that makes knowing genuine.

The next passage, one from James, is nothing less than a summary of Psalm 119. James 1:22-27 is a warning about Bible reading and theology as a discipline because it summarizes the entire Bible's thrust about what Scripture is for. Theology that is not lived is not theology.

But be doers of the word, and not merely hearers who deceive themselves. For if any are hearers of the word and not doers, they are like those who look at themselves in a mirror; for they look at themselves and, on going away, immediately forget what they were like. But those who look into the perfect law, the law of liberty, and persevere, being not hearers who forget but doers who act—they will be blessed in their doing.

If any think they are religious, and do not bridle their tongues but deceive their hearts, their religion is worthless. Religion that is pure and undefiled before God, the Father, is this: to care for orphans and widows in their distress, and to keep oneself unstained by the world.

The point of the word is doing the word, and those who think otherwise "deceive themselves." Accordingly, "Religion that is pure and undefiled before God" is not theology per se but theology lived out. How? "To care for orphans and widows in their distress" and as well "to keep oneself unstained by the world." Theology is designed for ethics. John Webster's lectures on the culture of theology finished with a lecture on nothing less than the character required for a theologian: "Good theology demands good theologians," he said more than once.[3] I'd like to ramp that up a bit to say that good theology demands theologians living good theology in such a way that their life is their theology.

FIVE RECENT PERSPECTIVES ON AN ETHICAL THEOLOGY

I turn now to five recent studies that confirm theology as lived theology, and each does so from the author's own discipline: New Testament studies, classic systematic theology, hermeneutical theology, Christian public ethics, and liberation theology. First, Ben Witherington's two-volume work on theological ethics or ethical theology was called *The Indelible Image* and is now retitled *New Testament Theology and Ethics*. Briefly, because Witherington and I are in the same discipline and I have said what he says already, I call attention here to his opening remarks about the shocking reality of New Testament theology as practiced today, asking, "Why is it that we Christians try

---

[3]John Webster, *The Culture of Theology*, ed. Ivor J. Davidson and Alden C. McCray (Grand Rapids, MI: Baker Academic, 2019), 131.

to isolate theology from the rest of what the New Testament is about—
history, ethics, praxis and related subjects?" He continues,

> But is there not an ethical dimension to New Testament the-
> ology and theologizing? . . . Are not ethics and theology in fact
> intertwined throughout the New Testament? Is there not both
> a theological basis and character to New Testament ethics and
> an ethical basis and character to New Testament theology? And
> after all, since all of the New Testament writers, or almost all of
> them, were Jews, why in the world would we think that they
> were not much more interested in orthopraxy, indeed as inter-
> ested in orthopraxy as orthodoxy? Take the teaching of Jesus,
> for instance. All those parables, aphorisms, maxims and stories
> have both a theological and an ethical character, edge and punch
> line. It seems that Jesus does not want us to talk about belief
> without also talking about behavior.[4]

This is worked out in two (long) volumes by Witherington, one focusing on individual witnesses to ethical theology and the other syn-
thesizing. Here is a New Testament theologian who sees the inte-
gration of theology and ethics in ways similar to what I am proposing.
How this works itself into a theology matters deeply.

Beth Felker Jones, a classic systematician, boldly titles her slim
systematics text *Practicing Christian Doctrine: An Introduction to
Thinking and Living Theologically.* I do not know of a systematics text
that focuses so clearly on practice. "Our beliefs," she states, "must be
put into practice"—which could put ethics into a separate category
in a topics frame, but she continues because she knows that ought
not to be done: "and faithful practice matters for what we believe."
Indeed. She knows the two are "intimately interconnected" and that
"doctrine and discipleship always go together." Perhaps what I like

---

[4]Ben W. Witherington III, *New Testament Theology and Ethics* (Downers Grove, IL: IVP
Academic, 2016), 1:14.

most about Jones's book, and I like it for many reasons, is that each chapter ends with a section on practicing a given topic or doctrine. In chapter four, "A Delightful World," which explores the doctrines of creation and providence, Jones concludes on her note of practice by observing that all of our life is about the doctrine of creation (work, play, marriage, sports [I added that last one]). She makes the astute observation that when "we become practiced in the doctrine of creation, we will find ourselves reoriented in life."[5] I here enumerate her list in quoting:

We will learn to turn, by the Spirit's power,

- from disdain for creation to Christian delight in its goodness;

- from the gnostic impulse to escapism to a commitment to presence and participation in the world;

- from proud attempts at meticulous control to grateful openness to God's work in our lives;

- from frustration with our finitude to appreciation of its graciousness;

- from fatalism and resignation to active involvement in God's world, fighting against sin and injustice;

- from doomed determination to be independent in all things to gratitude for our dependence on God and acceptance of interdependence with others;

- from despair over sin to awe of God's sovereignty and trust in God's purpose;

- from possessiveness to stewardship;

- from greed to giving;

- from abstemiousness to joy;

---

[5]Beth Felker Jones, *Practicing Christian Doctrine: An Introduction to Thinking and Living Theologically* (Grand Rapids, MI: Baker Academic, 2014), 2, 4, 95.

- from heeding the inner voice that calls us worthless to a new self-assurance that comes from the worth we have in God;

- from cynicism to a place where we cultivate the habit of wonder; and

- from entitlement to care of creation.[6]

These implications of the doctrine of creation integrate with the practice of creation integrating into a theology of creation. A lived theology of creation leads to reflection on our Creator and creaturely life. A theology of creation is to be lived if it is to be comprehended as God intends.

The next example of theology needing to be lived comes from hermeneutician Kevin Vanhoozer, whose large project called *The Drama of Doctrine* insightfully explores theology as something performed on the stage following the script called Scripture. Vanhoozer's mantle fell over the stage as his ruling metaphor, turning the gospel, theology, and Scripture into drama and script directed by a dramaturge (theologian) toward performance of the script. If his approach leans in the direction of a theology worked out in practice, it his emphasis on performance that I want to emphasize. "The church," he argues, "is a company of players gathered together to stage scenes of the kingdom of God for the sake of a watching world. The direction of doctrine thus enables us, as individuals and as a church, to render the gospel public by leading lives in creative imitation of Christ."[7] Here again, there is a theologian who, like Jones, does not leave theology as the three-article frame or topics frame of ideas expounded. He presses the ideas onto the stage where the life of the church and individual Christians embody the gospel.[8]

---

[6]Jones, *Practicing Christian Doctrine*, 95-96.
[7]Kevin J. Vanhoozer, *The Drama of Doctrine: A Canonical-Linguistic Approach to Christian Theology* (Louisville, KY: Westminster John Knox, 2005), 32-33.
[8]Another of his books develops all this with the metaphor of being trained in discipleship. See Kevin J. Vanhoozer, *Hearers and Doers: A Pastor's Guide to Making Disciples Through Scripture and Doctrine* (Bellingham, WA: Lexham, 2019). I have chosen to use his *Drama of Doctrine* here.

Fourth, Charles Marsh. I expound his view at more length because he approaches theology from the other end. Instead of beginning with ideas and seeing how they are done, practiced, or performed, he begins with the life of believers (practice, performance) to see the theology such a life signifies. Thus, Marsh offers for us a way of thinking about lived theology and, in doing so, challenges the all-too-common strategy approach that moves monodirectionally from theology (in the abstract) to practice (in the concrete). A brief sketch of his project at the University of Virginia deserves a mention. Marsh knows that what we *do* is not theologically neutral, so he observes, "Practices are inherently communicative, and, in the most basic sense, adhere to social settings and particular places." That is, what we do is not only not theologically neutral; it is often spatially determined or located. There is something, he observes, about actions that transcend ideas: "We might add that practices, theologically framed, overflow sacred events and sacred spaces, churches and congregations and religious actions and persons."[9] Marsh's term *practice* emerges in conversation with the ruling paradigm called virtue ethics. Alasdair MacIntyre defines virtue ethics but does the (verbal) twist in the process:

> By a "practice" I am going to mean any coherent and complex form of socially established cooperative human activity through which goods internal to that form of activity are realized in the course of trying to achieve those standards of excellence which are appropriate to, and partially definitive of, that form of activity, with the result that human powers to achieve excellence, and human conceptions of the ends and goods involved, are systematically extended.[10]

---

[9]Charles Marsh, Peter Slade, and Sarah Azaransky, eds., *Lived Theology: New Perspectives on Method, Style, and Pedagogy* (New York: Oxford University Press, 2016), 6-7.

[10]Alasdair MacIntyre, *After Virtue: A Study in Moral Theory*, 3rd ed. (Notre Dame, IN: University of Notre Dame Press, 2007), 187.

On virtue, he says all in italics: "A virtue is an acquired human quality the possession and exercise of which tends to enable us to achieve those goods which are internal to practices and the lack of which effectively prevents us from achieving any such goods."[11] Gordon Mikoski, in his sketch of practices in *The Dictionary of Scripture and Ethics*, defines *practices* in a manner more amenable to understanding: "observable phenomena of particular kinds of teleological human action in specific historical and communal contexts."[12]

Whether we think of practice as the overall way of life or as a particular constellation of one's way of life in a practice, or the even larger sense of lived theology from which we can infer a theology, Marsh provides for us an opportunity to think about theology as lived theology. We can infer from our life what theology is embodied. Marsh continues, "As such, lived theology is an apt expression for the foregrounding of embodied particularity in theological narrative." Marsh is not against theology, nor does he reduce theology to the phraseological (a Bonhoefferian expression). However, his quest is to apply theological method to theological living. So, he says, "Lived theology is therefore based on the rationale that the concrete forms of God's presence and action in the world promise rich and generative material for theological method, style, and pedagogy."[13] Marsh reminds us,

> The lack of a sense of place has quite often inhibited theology's narrative capabilities. Apropos of geographic influences on religious thought, Bonhoeffer would observe, in a letter written during his year as an assistant vicar in Barcelona, that his understanding of dogmatics and systematic theology had been "unsettled" by the strong impressions of Mediterranean culture.

---

[11]MacIntyre, *After Virtue*, 191.
[12]Gordon Mikoski, "Practices," in *The Dictionary of Scripture and Ethics*, ed. Joel B. Green et al. (Grand Rapids, MI: Baker Academic, 2011), 613.
[13]Marsh, Slade, and Azaransky, *Lived Theology*, 7-8.

"It's difficult to process them all," he wrote, "but one has become inescapable: Barth could not have written in Spain."[14]

And Romans was not written for Galatia, and neither of those letters would fit in Paul's trial before Felix in Caesarea Maritima or in Colossae. Marsh continues,

> Even as a clear *Sitz im Leben* proved generative in Bonhoeffer's contextual approach to writing and teaching, so in our collaborations [in Marsh's book], the right questions and a sense of place inspired a framework within which on-the-ground decisions regarding the interactions of theory and method became surprisingly uncomplicated. Absent a sense of place, we find ourselves lost in a no-man's land of concepts without footprints.[15]

Marsh thus evokes the significance of a located, specific community and tradition when it comes to virtues, practices, and lived theology.

Community then is vital for moral formation. The individualism of Rudolf Bultmann's famous indicative and imperative has been nuanced by David Horrell, who has argued in a number of settings that we are better off thinking not in terms of indicative and imperative but of *identity* formation in the context of community.[16] One of his conclusions is that identity formation occurs through comparison with other communities. Douglas Campbell's new *Pauline Dogmatics*, so rich in so many directions, is one of the very few I have read that overtly argues that we know God through our fellow humans. We meet God, Campbell says, through people who over time have become godly or godlike, which means location matters, people in location.[17]

[14]Marsh, Slade, and Azaransky, *Lived Theology*, 9.
[15]Marsh, Slade, and Azaransky, *Lived Theology*, 9.
[16]David G. Horrell, *Solidarity and Difference: A Contemporary Reading of Paul's Ethics*, 2nd ed. (London: Bloomsbury T&T Clark, 2015); Richard B. Hays, *The Moral Vision of the New Testament: Community, Cross, New Creation; A Contemporary Introduction to New Testament Ethics* (San Francisco: HarperOne, 1996), 99-115.
[17]Douglas A. Campbell, *Pauline Dogmatics: The Triumph of God's Love* (Grand Rapids, MI: Eerdmans, 2020), 57-62.

Fifth, the moment we think location, we think *our* location, and when we allow that we become alert to different locations forming into different theologies mediated by fellow humans in different locations. Latin American theologian Luis Pedraja draws on the now well-developed Latin American theologians who emphasized the divine preferential option for the poor and that soteriology must be connected to systemic liberation to be fully biblical—think Exodus. Pedraja contends, "That God comes to us in human form tells us something about God's revelation. It tells us that God's revelation does not occur *apart* from human experience. Rather, it occurs as *part* of it." He explores how the life Jesus lived reveals God:

> Thus we can conclude that Jesus' life exemplifies elements that are important to most people and to Hispanic life: faith, love, compassion, suffering, hope, and a desire for social change. By allowing us to compare our experiences with them, the characteristics we encounter in Jesus can serve as our guide for determining where and how God is present in humanity.

In a move now well known, he plays on the Spanish translations that have "the verb became flesh," and with these conclusions on the chalkboard he goes local into Iberian graphic suffering and tragedy as revelations of God.[18] Jesus' suffering for them is not morbidity or moroseness but the lived reality of Hispanic life. Touching on atonement theories, Pedraja also pushes back against many expiation and satisfaction theories to see in the cross of Jesus the exposure of injustice and that God is with us in our suffering. Theology is lived theology, and lived theology is local, and local experience then shapes theology.

Theology is embodied, and it is incomplete until it is embodied. One might say that ethics are the proving ground of the salience of our theology, and to tweak this one bit with some cheekiness, we

---

[18]Luis G. Pedraja, *Jesus Is My Uncle: Christology from a Hispanic Perspective* (Nashville: Abingdon, 1999), 40, 42, 60-84.

might say theology is the rationalization or at least rational exploration of our embodied practice. As such, ethics is not a topic late in
the frame but the governor for all the topics. It is not inaccurate to
observe that, when Jesus sat down to teach his disciples, what came
out of the Son's mouth was the Sermon on the Mount, not some
abstracted theology or a set of propositional truths. When the apostle
John does theology in 1 John, it is more about life, walking in the light,
avoiding darkness, abiding in Christ, and loving one's siblings than
about abstracted theology devoid of ethics. His theology was not a
set of ideas applied but a life of love and light intellectually explored.
When James gets down to work, his letter is an exercise in Jesus-
shaped ethics that must be lived. So this final chapter turns to an
exposition of Romans 12:1-2 as lived theology that seeks to illustrate
the whole agenda of this book.

LIVED THEOLOGY IN ROMANS

Many, if not most, think Romans 1:16-17 is the theme of Romans.
There are good reasons to think this, especially if we follow the theological trajectory set for reading the letter in the history of the church.
Here are those verses: "For I am not ashamed of the gospel; it is the
power of God for salvation to everyone who has faith, to the Jew first
and also to the Greek. For in it the righteousness of God is revealed
through faith for faith; as it is written, 'The one who is righteous will
live by faith.'" There you have it for many. Romans is about the gospel,
the gospel is about salvation for all, and it's about righteousness by
faith (or justification by faith).

But there are reasons to wonder whether it's all that simple, and
we are right back where we have been: thinking these verses are the
theme of Romans is once again the privileging of topics with ethics,
and lived theology is gasping for some air in its wake. So I join the
minority who either argue there is no such thing as a theme set of
verses or who think we ought to look to Romans 12:1-2 to get the

theme of Romans: "I appeal to you therefore, brothers and sisters, by the mercies of God, to present your bodies as a living sacrifice, holy and acceptable to God, which is your spiritual worship. Do not be conformed to this world, but be transformed by the renewing of your minds, so that you may discern what is the will of God—what is good and acceptable and perfect."

There is no way to adjudicate which verses in Romans are the most important, so I want to drop this conversation right where it is: perhaps Romans 1:16-17 is not the theme, and perhaps Romans 12:1-2 is, and perhaps we ought not to argue about it because there's no way to decide. I do want to say that these latter two verses ought to be given weight in any reading of Romans. This is what Paul, after all, is aiming at in his letter, and I will make these verses the focus of our attention in what follows.

Strategies and tactics. Some interpretations of Romans 12:1-2 are anodyne and offer bromides to unsuspecting pew sitters, as in "Let's sacrifice our vacation this year to help the poor in Mexico." But the everyday life of ordinary followers of Jesus in Rome who followed Paul's offensive teachings was anything but anodyne. That kind of life, describable as everyday sacrifice, was radical and subversive. To use the terms of Michel de Certeau, a life of everyday sacrifice was in fact a "tactic" by the powerless that subverted the "strategies" of the Roman powerful.[19] Subversion was required—correct that, it was the only option—because the agent (Rome) was so powerful. Romans 12:1-2 can be seen as a tactic to subvert Rome's strategies.

Rome per se was perhaps not Paul's target. Sin and the Flesh at work in the Roman way of life were. Sin and the Flesh, two terms turned feeble in much Christian rhetoric, were ruining the fellowship of the strong and weak in Rome. Sin and Flesh in Pauline discourse are not reducible to conditions or simple actions but are active agents

---

[19]Michel de Certeau, *The Practice of Everyday Life*, trans. Steven Rendall (Berkeley: University of California Press, 1984), xix, 34-39.

(hence uppercase is appropriate), as Matthew Croasmun's stunning new work on the use of emergence theory to examine the cosmic tyrant of sin amply shows.[20] Romans 12:1-2, then, should be seen as a tactic against Sin and the Flesh at work in the house churches in Rome (Rom 14–15; more below). What we find in our passage is not, to use the words of Robert Jewett, "vaguely uplifting sentiments," but an earthy, demanding, sacrificial life known only in the hardships those challenges created.[21] This everyday sacrifice is not just a moral idea or an ethical vision but, as Kavin Rowe has argued, one true life that rivals various Roman traditions and is known by its practices or lived theology.[22]

Before I seek to show that biblical theology works into a lived theology as a climax of what theology is all about, I want to sketch a common reading of these verses that fails to rise to the level of everyday sacrifice as a tactic that subverts the Roman way of life, its strategy for sustaining and retaining its one true life. This sketch will provide for us a way of seeing theology as located in the next portion of the chapter.

Reading Romans 12:1-2 as a Christendom strategy. Theology begins with biblical reflection, and going back to the Bible is required for us to become responsible Christian theologians. It is not necessary here to delve into deep exegesis, and I will hold footnotes to a minimum, but I call to attention eight observations about this text. Again, here's the text: "I appeal to you therefore, brothers and sisters, by the mercies of God, to present your bodies as a living sacrifice, holy and acceptable to God, which is your spiritual worship. Do not be conformed to this world, but be transformed by the renewing of your minds, so that you may discern what is the will of God—what is good and acceptable and perfect."

---

[20]Matthew Croasmun, *The Emergence of Sin: The Cosmic Tyrant in Romans* (New York: Oxford University Press, 2017).

[21]Robert Jewett, *Romans: A Commentary*, Hermeneia (Minneapolis: Fortress, 2007), 728.

[22]C. Kavin Rowe, *One True Life: The Stoics and Early Christians as Rival Traditions* (New Haven, CT: Yale University Press, 2016).

I will begin with the observation that the *therefore* of Romans 12:1 has generated the question of whether the exhortation is the logical consequence of Romans 1:1 to Romans 11:33, with some emphasizing Romans 5–8, or the consequence only of Romans 9–11, with emphasis on the theme of mercy in Romans 11:30-32. It seems best that it is because of God's mercy in Christ to form a redeemed people of *both* Jews and Gentiles that the believers in Rome are exhorted ("therefore") to offer themselves as a sacrifice.

Second, Paul's exhortation to the baptized-into-Christ's-death Roman Christians is that they are "to present [their] bodies as a living sacrifice," which is then clarified in Romans 12:2 as a reciprocating, complementing, and alternating double: "do not be *conformed* to this world" and "be *transformed*." The Christian life is one rooted in the cross and resurrection of Christ, one of participation in that Christ event, and thus also one of world denial and mental-moral transformation.[23] The term *present* here recapitulates what Paul said in Romans 6 about presenting our bodies for righteousness (see, e.g., Rom 12:13, 16, 19). *Third*, the offering to be made is an *embodied* offering ("your bodies"). Paul exhorts the believers to surrender their living, breathing, vibrant bodies all day long—in relationships, in communications, in business, in all things. Since he does not have in mind a cloistered life or spiritual-but-not-embodied existence, we have here groundwork for one's vocation as the location for one's sacrifice. As Ernst Käsemann suggests, all of life thus becomes worship.[24] *Fourth*, Paul hereby expands what sacrifice and temple mean, and locates the latter in the house churches and the former in Christ's death and Eucharist.[25] To pick up an observation not developed in

[23]Michael J. Gorman, *Becoming the Gospel: Paul, Participation, and Mission* (Grand Rapids, MI: Eerdmans, 2015), 26-36.
[24]Ernst Käsemann, *Commentary on Romans* (Grand Rapids, MI: Eerdmans, 1980), 325-31.
[25]E.g., 1 Cor 3:16-17; 6:19; 2 Cor 6:16, both reaching back to words of Jesus (Mk 14:58). For discussion, see James D. G. Dunn, *The Theology of Paul the Apostle* (Grand Rapids, MI: Eerdmans, 1998), 545-47.

the previous point above, Richard Hays notes that the plural term *bodies* evokes not individual Christian living but ecclesial life. What is said in Romans 12:1-2, then, "must be performed by the community as a whole." Hays continues with, "God transforms and saves a *people*, not atomized individuals. Consequently, the faithful find their identity and vocation in the world as the body of Christ."[26]

Fifth, this is, Paul says, your "spiritual worship," a translation that has earned a million grumbles. The NRSV's "spiritual worship" corresponds to the NIV's "true and proper worship" and the CEB's "appropriate priestly service." Everything hinges on *logikos*, a term used but once by the apostle Paul but found throughout his world for what is reasonable and rational and logical, thus leading to translation suggestions such as "rational religion" and "reasonable worship."[27] Most today know Paul could have used *pneumatikos* had he meant "spiritual," so we are left to ponder a different sense from "spiritual." Barclay again takes us one step closer to the prize: the reasonableness here is not simply rationality but "newly defined by the act of God in Christ," and "the logic controlling the Christian *habitus* is self-consciously at odds with the prevailing logics of contemporary society."[28] A *logikē* worship, I add, never loses connection with the *logos*.[29] Thus, this calculated or reasonable worship is embodied Christology or, better yet, Christoformity.

Sixth, Romans 12:2, as stated earlier, explicates Romans 12:1 with a double vision: not being conformed but being transformed. The NRSV's, NIV's, and CEB's "this world" mask the Greek expression *tō aiōni toutō*, which rendered literally would be "this age" or "this era." Translating it as "world" suggests the term is *kosmos*, which it isn't, and

---

[26]Hays, *Moral Vision*, 36, emphasis original.

[27]For good discussion, see esp. Craig S. Keener, *The Mind of the Spirit: Paul's Approach to Transformed Thinking* (Grand Rapids, MI: Baker Academic, 2016), 150-52.

[28]John M. G. Barclay, *Paul and the Gift* (Grand Rapids, MI: Eerdmans, 2015), 509 and n28.

[29]Sarah Heaner Lancaster, *Romans*, Belief: A Theological Commentary on the Bible (Louisville, KY: Westminster John Knox, 2015), 205.

also avoiding "era" or "age" avoids the temporal register in which this Greek term is found. *Seventh*, the order not to be conformed— *syschēmatizō*—stands alongside 1 Corinthians 7:31's "For the present form [*schēma*] of this world is passing away," and this pushes the meaning of *tō aiōni toutō* decisively away from "this world" to "this age" or "this era." This is a term expressing apostolic eschatology more than apostolic cosmology, and as such touches on the philosophical tradition in Stoicism but even more the apocalyptic act of God in Christ.[30] *Eighth*, the alternative, the complement, the reciprocation of saying no to this age's powers, is saying yes to a revival or renewal— by God's grace through the Spirit. Both grace and Spirit are dominant enough in Romans to state that the renewal is God's work.[31] This metamorphosis completes repentance. Grace and Spirit need to be strengthened with attention to the unleashing of resurrection powers, as well as with the ascension, from which status the Son sent the Spirit, who regenerates with grace, to comprehend Paul's sense of metamorphosis here. This sense of metamorphosis partakes as well in Paul's inaugurated eschatology. As the idolater's mind is "debased" (Rom 1:28) so it needs renewal, surely a complement to 1 Corinthians 2:16's "we have the mind of Christ."[32] Tying a few of these observations now together, the sacrifice of one's embodied existence is a person's Christoform, reasonable worship and manifests itself in both disentangling oneself from this age's powers and in entangling oneself in a mental renewal. This leads to an ability to "discern what is the will of God—what is good and acceptable and perfect" (Rom 12:2).

Very few make Paul's words here anything other than a bromide, a comfortable *strategy* for Christian living in general. One example is

---

[30]On New Testament eschatology, see Craig L. Blomberg, *A New Testament Theology* (Waco, TX: Baylor University Press, 2018). For this passage's resonances, see Keener, *Mind of the Spirit*, 156-58.

[31]For discussions, see Barclay, *Paul and the Gift*; Gordon Fee, *God's Empowering Presence: The Holy Spirit in the Letters of Paul* (Peabody, MA: Hendrickson, 1994).

[32]For full analysis, see Keener, *Mind of the Spirit*, 143-72.

Joseph Fitzmyer, who summarizes our passage in this way: "In this way he sees the transformation or metamorphosis of the Christian that has taken place as an effect of the Christ event working itself out in concrete everyday life."[33] However, one who digs into Roman realities, and thus suggests these verses as a subversive *tactic*, is Robert Jewett: "A sacrifice killed or burned on the altar is hardly the appropriate metaphor for mopping the floor." And further, "To list the 'good and acceptable and perfect' in the context of nonconformity with this world and of determining the will of God is to legitimize as well as challenge the behavioral standards of the various groups of Roman believers and the cultural arenas from which they were drawn."[34]

A much-needed and jarring cry jumps off the page in Sarah Lancaster's study of Romans:

> In this letter directed to a specific audience, Paul is exhorting a specific group of people about specific problems, not setting out general counsels for all Christians in all times. . . . Leading these exhortations as timeless, general counsels actually makes them less valuable to us because we bypass the specific reasoning Paul used to understand how life before God should be lived.[35]

Some exegesis lacks attention to specific historical contexts. Too easily in this kind of reading, Romans 12:1-2 becomes an endorsement of Christendom, of our local brand of our national brand of our ecumenical brand of Christianity. Our embodied sacrifice does not subvert the world, the Flesh, or Sin and instead thinks it dodges them as they continue to pervade our midst. Instead of subverting privilege, that claimed by both the strong and the weak in Rome, it talks another language. Instead of living in Christ, we live in the self; instead of finding peace among the siblings in Christ, we

---

[33]J. A. Fitzmyer, *Romans*, Anchor Yale Bible Commentary 33 (New Haven, CT: Yale University Press, 2007), 639.
[34]Jewett, *Romans*, 728, 735.
[35]Lancaster, *Romans*, 201.

carry on with our disunities with utter tranquility or perhaps a vague
wish that things were different; instead of eating with enemies and
converting them into neighbors, we eat with one anothers who are
as much alike as any social club in North America; and instead of
reciprocating in spiritual gifts, we use ours and expect others to
become like us or to exalt us. No, embodied sacrifice can fall well
short if it is not seen as a tactic of subverting the world, Sin, and the
Flesh—Rome, in concrete specifics.

What, concretely, did Paul have in mind with this image of everyday sacrifice? To use one of J. Christiaan Beker's memorable expressions, what do these verses look like when we focus them on "the
historical particularity of Paul's situational theology"?[36] Surely Paul's
image had more feet and legs and fingers and toes than generalized
ethical admonitions. The more generalized reading of Romans 12:1-2
is a *strategy* in de Certeau's terms, which means seeing embodied
sacrifice as acts by those in power that consciously or unconsciously
prop up that power. We can explore the same passage in another of
de Certeau's terms, namely, that Romans 12:1-2 is a *tactic* for the
marginalized. As a tactic, which is a behavior by one not in power, by
one who is the other, by one in subalternity, and for the sake of
subversion—as a tactic, what Paul says is subversive, but just as the
theology of Romans 1–11 is not "dogmatic monologue," so his appeal
in Romans 12:1-2 is not a general, abstract call to subversion or to be
subversives in the sense of a principle.[37] Romans 12:1-2 is a call to
subversion in a particular time and place.[38]

Reading Romans as a tactic of subversion: Back to the Bible. A
tactic, to quote de Certeau, is "an art of the weak."[39] For many,

---

[36]J. Christiaan Beker, *Paul the Apostle: The Triumph of God in Life and Thought* (Philadelphia:
Fortress, 1982), 64.

[37]"Dogmatic monologue" comes from Beker, *Paul the Apostle*, 64.

[38]A parallel set of observations can be seen in an insightful study of the tactics of Jews/Judeans
in their various contexts of oppression by Steven Weitzman, *Surviving Sacrilege: Cultural
Persistence in Jewish Antiquity* (Cambridge, MA: Harvard University Press, 2005).

[39]De Certeau, *Practice of Everyday Life*, 37.

Romans 1–8, or Romans 1–11, is pure theology, while Romans 12–16 is ethics, praxis, the impure. Lived theology does not subordinate *lived* to the pure *theology*, so maybe one could say Romans 12–16 is the theological life of Romans. One could perhaps say Romans 1–11 rationalizes Romans 12–16. Which is why more need to read Romans 12–16 before reading Romans 1–11. One of my students, Ben Davis, suggested that what we find in Romans is a call *to live into a new way of thinking*. In Miroslav Volf and Matthew Croasmun's book *For the Life of the World*, we are treated to an argument for the conviction that theology, while it is grounded in God and redemption, is about a flourishing life.[40] That, too, is an example of learning to see Romans 12–16 not as application of the pure theology of Romans 1–11 but as the point of the whole letter.

Reading Romans backward, first outlined in a short book by Paul Minear, is a needed approach for at least two reasons: if readers today are not worn out by the time they get to Romans 9:1, they are by the time they get to Romans 12:1.[41] Surely Romans is what Peter had in mind when he said, "There are some things in them hard to understand" (2 Pet 3:16). The second reason is that Romans is so long and involved, and the audience so clarified in Romans 12–16, that combining them is necessary. One can read deeply into common commentaries as well as intense studies on Romans before one hears anything about the audience described in Romans 12–16. Which is to say, Romans 12:1-2 must be read in light of Romans 12–16, especially Romans 14–15, where Paul talks about the weak and the strong, in order to convert our two verses from strategy into tactic. What has happened is that Romans has become theology in

---

[40]Miroslav Volf and Matthew Croasmun, *For the Life of the World: Theology That Makes a Difference* (Grand Rapids, MI: Brazos, 2019), esp. 61-83.

[41]Paul S. Minear, *The Obedience of Faith: The Purposes of Paul in the Epistle to the Romans*, Studies in Biblical Theology 2.19 (London: SCM Press, 1971); Scot McKnight, *Reading Romans Backwards: A Gospel of Peace in the Midst of Empire* (Waco, TX: Baylor University Press, 2019).

an abstract sense and Romans 12:1-2 has become a theoretical approach to applying Romans 1–11.

But when we read Romans through the lens of the weak-and-strong issue of Romans 14–15, we turn from Romans in the abstract to Romans in the real. This letter was written by a real apostle to a real group of house churches, probably at least five: the households/house churches of

1. Prisca and Aquila (Rom 16:3-5)

2. slaves of Aristobulus (Rom 16:10)

3. slaves of Narcissus (Rom 16:11)

4. brothers with Asyncritus (Rom 16:14)

5. the saints with Philologus (Rom 16:15)

Furthermore, the situation in Rome was complicated not only by a Jewish origin for the church in Rome but an attempted destruction of that movement when Claudius sent the Jews, or perhaps better Jewish Christians, away. This led to a more Gentile center to the church, and until the Jewish believers returned, the Gentile culture of the Christian movement in Rome became dominant, leading to cultural tensions between the Jewish and Gentile believers in Rome when the former returned in the early years of Nero. Paul weighs in on this with labels that no doubt provoked as much as clarified: the Jewish believers he calls weak and the Gentile believers he calls strong. The situation is more complex than this, for it appears that Paul may well have seen himself as one of the strong, or at least at times his own views overlapped with theirs. In general, though, strong is about the privileged Gentile believers and the weak about Jewish believers who claimed elective privilege in God's plan.

Among the house churches in Rome, then, there was a battle of the privileged: Gentile Roman believers with social status who had power in their privilege against Jewish believers with no social status who had no power but were loaded with elective privilege, which is one of the complicating themes of Romans 9–11. Romans 15:1 may express this most succinctly: "We who are strong ought to put up with the failings of the weak, and not to please ourselves." Or, put in more sociologically labeling terms: "We, the *dynatoi* (the powerful), ought to shoulder the weaknesses of the *a-dynatoi* (the powerless)— that is, we ought not to be pleasing ourselves and making things go our own way."

Who then were the weak and who were the strong? Here is my sketch: The *weak* are Jewish believers who are in the stream of God's election and need to be affirmed in their election but who have questions about the faithfulness of God to that election and who need to embrace the surprising moves of God throughout Israel's history. The weak know the Torah, practice the Torah, but in the person of the Judge (of Rom 2) sit in judgment on Gentiles, especially the strong in the Christian community in Rome, even though the weak have no status or privilege or power. Furthermore, the weak are tempted to resist paying taxes to Rome on the basis of the Jewish zealotry tradition (Rom 13:1-7). In addition, the weak—in the face of the Judge— need to apply faith in Christ more radically to themselves, so discovering that they are a new example of the remnant of Israel, and they need to see that the sufficiency of faith means that Gentile believers in Christ are siblings so they can see that Torah observance is not the way of transformation for either themselves or the strong in Rome.

The *strong* are predominately Gentiles who believe in Jesus as Messiah or king, who do not observe Torah as the will of God for them and who have condescending and despising attitudes probably toward Jews but especially to Jewish believers in Jesus, and all of this is wrapped up in the superior higher status of the strong in Rome. Paul and Jewish believers who embrace the nonnecessity of Torah observance are at least at times among the strong in their theological convictions about Torah observance as the way of Christoformity.

But the strong are taking advantage of their superior social status to denigrate the Torah and holiness as the quest of the Christians in Rome, and so they are coercing the weak into table fellowship over nonkosher food. The strong are as known for their position on observance of Torah and for their status as they are for ethnicity.

To cut to the goal now: Romans 12:1-2 is a thematic statement designed to speak exclusively to the weak and the strong. It is not a simple, abstract Christian living statement but a concrete expression of how two sides of a debate in Rome, who are at each other's throats, can learn to express unity in Christ by becoming Christoform in how they relate to one another and how they can learn to embody fellowship with one another. There is a newness at work in Romans 12:1-2 that can only be called apocalyptic.

A tactical reading of Romans 12:1-2. These verses are addressed, as all of Romans is, to Christians in Rome, weak and strong, but still Christians. They are marginal. Words such as these spoken to people such as these are not going to be heard as soothing moral sentiments but as demanding, as challenging, and as subversions of the Roman and Jewish way of life. To tell the weak to die—for that is what it means to "present your bodies as a living sacrifice"—is not a call to comfort. It is to tell the strong that their status no longer matters. It is to tell them their condescending, insufferable, self-righteous actions are to cease. It is to tell them to be sensitive to the food scruples of their Jewish siblings in Christ. It is to tell them to sit at the table "but not for the purpose of quarreling over opinions" (Rom 14:1). It is to tell them that their *dynatoi*-life is the Roman way of life and not Christoform and cruciform. It is to tell them that the story of Israel, updated to include their presence as genuine descendants of Abraham, is now their story. Forget *The Iliad* and *The Odyssey*, known as the Greek old and new testaments; forget the Roman bible, Virgil's *Aeneid*; embrace the LXX as your story. It is to tell them they are not to look down on but to look up to their Jewish siblings.

Read in context, Romans 12:1-2 tells the weak their privilege remains by election, by grace, but only by faith in Jesus as their Messiah. It is to affirm them while also challenging them to embrace the surprising ways of God in history that now include the surprising belief of Gentiles and a surprising, correlating rejection by some of their kin. It is to tell them God is faithful but in surprising ways. Thus, it is to tell them to die to some dimensions of their story and embrace other dimensions of that story of Israel. It is to tell them that Torah observance is not the way of transformation. It is to tell them that all along transformation has happened by God's grace, God's sovereign ways, God's surprising gift of the Spirit. It is to tell them to die to judging Gentiles and Gentile believers. It is to tell them that kosher food is not required for Gentile believers and that they can sit at table with each other. It is to tell them to tolerate differences over what Jewett calls "leafy vegetables." Without defense at this point, it is to tell them to pay their taxes and not to use the tactics of the Zealots. It is to tell them to accept that faith, as the true response to God's grace in Christ, is all that is needed, and that anything behind, below, above, or in front of that squashes the generosity of God's grace.

The death to which Paul calls the Roman Christians, then, is the death of privilege, and it is the embrace of siblings as equals in the one family of God. The privileged strong are to surrender their status as the privileged weak surrender their status too. This is a call to death of their past and to what Paul calls at about the same time "new creation" (2 Cor 5:17).

When Paul says "present your *bodies*," something else emerges from the weak-and-strong context. Jewett has argued the case that many if not most of those mentioned in Romans 16 are slave names from slave households, even tenement households. Peter Oakes insightfully argues that if we read Romans 14–15 in the context of a typical household in Pompeii and, with some adjustments, in Rome, this term *body* will refer in many cases to slave bodies turning their bodies away from their masters toward a new Lord, a new God, and a new family, the church.[42] In that context there is not to be abuse of the body and degradation of the body, but there is to be an honoring, a sanctifying, and an elevation of the body as beautiful and made in God's image. If we slip into a different register, these are words for Jewish and Gentile bodies, believers, whose bodies will not be mixed—in fellowship, in worship, in marriage—with bodies formerly verboten or at least restricted. To give and receive spiritual gifts is highlighted in Romans 12:3-8, but there is a noticeable emphasis there again on the body. To eat with one another at the same table is the clearest instruction of Paul's in Romans 14–15. Romans 14:1's imperative for the strong to welcome the weak is followed by instructions for eating with one another and transgressing boundaries previously obeyed. Romans 15:7 turns this into *mutual* welcome, and thus into mutual table fellowship. It works both ways for Paul.

Think about this realistically, which is what theology as lived theology is. It is not comforting to summon folks in our churches to sit down with those in the other political party, on the opposite side of the fence economically, or with differing moral positions, especially if one is told not to argue but to talk about things in common. It is, to summarize for both groups, to learn what Paul states in Romans 14:17: "For the kingdom of God is not food and drink but righteousness and peace and joy in the Holy Spirit." Katherine Grieb gets this exactly right:

> The embodiedness of our existence functions as a demonstration of the power of the gospel in and over its messengers. What we do with our lives, our embodied existence and the materiality of daily decision making, inevitably reveals the extent of the lordship of Jesus Christ in our lives. To the degree that the living Lord has drawn us into a new sphere of power,

---

[42]Peter Oakes, *Reading Romans in Pompeii: Paul's Letter at Ground Level* (Minneapolis: Fortress, 2009).

the powers of the present age lose their ability to conform us to the world. Christians no longer "belong" to these powers because their bodies have been offered as a living sacrifice to God and belong to God as the body of Jesus Christ.[43]

Charles Marsh, whose lived theology project inspired some of this chapter, contends that the stories of our lives are every bit as much theologies as our so-called purer theological systems. Those who die to their privilege—strong and weak—tell a story of death. R. H. Fuller's famous translation of Bonhoeffer's *The Cost of Discipleship* led to wording more poetic than Bonhoeffer's and far more memorable: "When Jesus bids a man come, he bids him come and die." Bonhoeffer's words were not so poetic: *Jeder Ruf Jesu führt zum Tod*, which translated is, "Every summons of Jesus leads to death."[44] To "present your bodies as a living sacrifice" is Paul's expression of what became Bonhoeffer's, one that carries forward Jesus' own summons to take up the cross. If one of the privileged strong or privileged weak died like this, they would have embodied Romans 6. Lived theology, however, asks us to turn this around: Romans 6 explicates a strong or weak believer dying to self for the good of the other. Romans 6 is derivable from the *habitus* of Romans 12:1. Romans 6 was generated in Paul's missionary work with Jewish and Gentile believers as he worked out their salvation with them, as he worked out fellowship in churches made up of wholly different folks. Romans 6 maps onto Romans 12:1-2 as Romans 12:1-2 maps onto Romans 6. It works both ways, and one suspects that Romans 12 prompted Romans 6 as much, if not more, as vice versa.

Reading Romans 12:1-2 theologically. The purpose of everyday sacrifices of the body is not spiritual ecstasies but the capacity to do

---

[43]A. Katherine Grieb, *The Story of Romans: A Narrative Defense of God's Righteousness* (Louisville, KY: Westminster John Knox, 2002), 119.

[44]Dietrich Bonhoeffer, *Discipleship*, Dietrich Bonhoeffer Works 4 (Minneapolis: Fortress, 2001), 87; see n11 for the R. H. Fuller translation.

what is good, what is approved by God, and what completes itself in a Christoform way of life. What might that be? Once again, read in context and read as a tactic of subverting the Roman and nonbelieving Jewish ways of life, this will entail at least the following four observations. Again, these are tactics of the underground designed to subvert the Roman way of life in the house churches of Rome.

First, a renewed mind approves *Christoformity*. Michael Gorman has developed a line of thinking called cruciformity, or conformity to the cross, and I agree with him but prefer the term *Christoformity*. Christoformity is a conformity of our lives to Christ as a person in all his person and work or, with a hat tip to the Barthian and Torrancian scholars, a participation in Christ. Thus, it is—to coin bad terms— bio-formity, cruci-formity, and anastasi-formity. Whatever one calls it, it bleeds through these chapters.

> We do not live to ourselves, and we do not die to ourselves. If we live, we live to the Lord, and if we die, we die to the Lord; so then, whether we live or whether we die, we are the Lord's. For to this end Christ died and lived again, so that he might be Lord of both the dead and the living. (Rom 14:7-9)

> If your brother or sister is being injured by what you eat, you are no longer walking in love. Do not let what you eat cause the ruin of one for whom Christ died. (Rom 14:15)

> The one who thus serves Christ is acceptable to God and has human approval. (Rom 14:18)

> For Christ did not please himself; but, as it is written, "The insults of those who insult you have fallen on me." (Rom 15:3)

> May the God of steadfastness and encouragement grant you to live in harmony with one another, in accordance with Christ Jesus. (Rom 15:5)

> Welcome one another, therefore, just as Christ has welcomed you, for the glory of God. For I tell you that Christ has become

a servant of the circumcised on behalf of the truth of God in order that he might confirm the promises given to the patriarchs. (Rom 15:7-8)

To be like Christ, then, is to die to ourselves, to live for God, to die to our food preferences since Christ died for both sides, to embrace anyone who serves Christ, to die to our self-pleasing and to embrace pleasing others, to live in harmony, to welcome one another, and to engage in the Gentile mission. Christoformity is the driving theme for Christian behavior; it is the warrant and the canon.

Second, a renewed mind approves *unity*. From what I have said, this is redundant, but it bears repeating: Paul desires that the tension between the strong and weak collapse into unity in Christ. Since God is the judge of all (Rom 14:4) and since Christ died for all (Rom 14:9, 15), they are to welcome one another. Since God's gifts are distributed to each for the good of the other, they are to dwell in unity. Since they are to live in love (Rom 12:9-10), they are to "live in harmony with one another" and not appeal to their status (Rom 12:16) and to "live peaceably with all" (Rom 12:18), all illustrated in being good social members and paying taxes (Rom 13:1-7). The strong and the weak, then, are to have the kind of renewed mind that pursues peace with all.

Third, a renewed mind approves *eating with another*. This theme features more in Jewett's work than most but also in Reta Finger's varied works.[45] Eating is embodied fellowship; it is embodied unity; it is embodied tolerance; it is embodied peace. Romans 14:1-6 is shaped by this theme as the way a renewed mind works, even if modern readers routinely ask, "But what about?" questions. "Some judge one day to be better than another, while others judge all days to be alike. Let all be fully convinced in their own minds. Those who observe the day, observe it in honor of the Lord. Also those who eat,

---

[45]Jewett, *Romans*; Reta Halteman Finger, *Roman House Churches for Today: A Practical Guide for Small Groups* (Grand Rapids, MI: Eerdmans, 2007).

eat in honor of the Lord, since they give thanks to God; while those who abstain, abstain in honor of the Lord and give thanks to God" (Rom 14:5-6). Fair enough, one says. But what do the weak think of this tactic for unity? Others wonder about Romans 14:17's famous words: "For the kingdom of God is not food and drink but righteousness and peace and joy in the Holy Spirit." But what about kosher food laws? Drop them? Keep them? Even more questions arise when one reads to "resolve instead never to put a stumbling block or hindrance in the way of another" (Rom 14:13).

That can go both ways. When Paul says "nothing is unclean" (Rom 14:14), he has undeniably cut through most of these questions and given clarity to Romans 14:7's famous words. But his point, too, is don't force yourself on another; let each person grow into maturity on these topics—and at their own pace. Christoform denial becomes a heavy word here: "Everything is indeed clean, but it is wrong for you to make others fall by what you eat; it is good not to eat meat or drink wine or do anything that makes your brother or sister stumble" (Rom 14:20-21). His final parting shot on the issue of eating with another is "whatever does not proceed from faith is sin" (Rom 14:23). #kerplunk, and now watch the ripples. A renewed mind eats with another, challenging and wrinkled as this may be.

Fourth, a renewed mind *reciprocates with spiritual gifts*. Romans 5–8 is the core of Romans when it comes to living in Christ. Romans 5–8 rationalizes the kind of Christian community envisioned in Romans 12–16. At the heart of Paul's words, words that immediately follow Romans 12:1-2, are words about life in the Spirit. I repeat them:

> For by the grace given to me I say to everyone among you not to think of yourself more highly than you ought to think, but to think with sober judgment, each according to the measure of faith that God has assigned. For as in one body we have many members, and not all the members have the same function, so we, who are many, are one body in Christ, and individually we

are members one of another. We have gifts that differ according to the grace given to us: prophecy, in proportion to faith; ministry, in ministering; the teacher, in teaching; the exhorter, in exhortation; the giver, in generosity; the leader, in diligence; the compassionate, in cheerfulness. (Rom 12:3-8)

Paul's themes in spiritual gifts teaching are well known. Each is or has a gift; each exercises the gift for the other; exercising gifts and receiving gifts creates reciprocity and even obligation; the gifts draw people into a unity. This unity is the harmonious body of Christ. A renewed mind reciprocates with spiritual gifts.

TRUE THEOLOGY IS EMBODIED

Kavin Rowe, in his splendid *One True Life*, mounts a lengthy and eloquent defense of approaching the Christian faith vis-à-vis the Stoic way of life in these bold terms:

> Trust, induction, discipline, instruction, formation, apprenticeship, care, healing—these were the ways the truth of all things was known and thought. Not this or that piece of information about the human condition, not this or that view of the *pneuma* (spirit/air), not this or that take on the passions, but an existentially structuring pattern, a trajectory of living the one and only life we can live in the midst of time; this was the way truth was contested. . . . The difference the names Stoic and Christian represent is thus lived truth.

His conclusion is, "True wisdom is the repair of reason by trust in the trustworthiness of the Crucified Christ—what looks to the world's way of knowing to be pure folly."[46] To think about Romans in this context, then, the acts of the strong and weak toward one another, *their lived theology of welcoming one another,* if they are acts

---

[46]Rowe, *One True Life*, 6, 7, 221. A good summary is found on 237.

of embodied sacrifices for the good of the other, will overflow both Romans 6 and Romans 12 in ways that communicate something more than those texts.

Lauren Winner, in her newest book that takes on virtue ethics and habits, *The Dangers of Christian Practice*, contends that habits are neither neutral nor always formational. She contends in some contexts what was meant for good and for spiritual benefit can become nasty *de*formations. MacIntyre himself said, "Where the virtues are required, the vices also may flourish."[47] Turning Romans 12:1-2 from the realm of strategies to tactics does not redeem embodied sacrifice. Why? Sin and Flesh as agents, to get to the point. Winner puts it this way: "Sin is what's ushered in by the Fall and produces all this damage. That is, the word *sin* denotes habits, actions, and proclivities of human beings (and other creatures with agency, such as angels and perhaps certain other nonhuman primates) that draw what God created away from God and that unleash damage into the world."[48]

If this is the world in which we live, our practices—our embodied sacrifices in the everyday life as a tactic of world subversion—can become sullied with Sin and Flesh, and Winner continues: "Things become deformed by sin in ways that are proper to the thing being deformed, and when those deformations have consequences, you cannot separate the consequences from the deformed thing itself, because it belongs to the thing potentially to have those very consequences." One of her many illustrations cuts to the bone: "It is characteristic of modern academia that its participants get corrupted by pride; pride is a corruption that tells us something about what academia is." So Winner explores three practices, beginning with Eucharist, which at times became the opportunity for some Christians to murder Jews for murdering Jesus. Then prayer in the hands of slave

---

[47]MacIntyre, *After Virtue*, 193.
[48]Lauren F. Winner, *The Dangers of Christian Practice: On Wayward Gifts, Characteristic Damage, and Sin* (New Haven, CT: Yale University Press, 2018), 2.

owners became "commandeering petitionary prayer" or "the wagon with which one keeps circling around a misbegotten object of desire," including damnation of one's slaves while purportedly praying for their redemption. Finally, baptism, which she shows was done at times in private homes with only family present, can become a celebration of social status and economic privilege divorced from church and community.[49]

What deformations arise when we turn Romans 12:1-2 from the world of strategy to the world of tactic? When embodied everyday sacrifice is detached

from Christoformity,

from unity and peace with one another,

from eating with one another,

and from reciprocations of spiritual gifts,

it becomes instead a strategy

that mocks the cross and Christ,

that destroys unity and peace with self-satisfied congratulations of piety,

of a division of hierarchies, with one's own insufferable self-righteousness at the top peering down on the others,

and with spiritual gifts not as reciprocating graces but as offices and stations and locations where we perceive ourselves as superior because of what ironically we have been given by the one who gave it all.

This kind of life is what theology is, so any theology that does not embody this kind of life is not theology. Theology is to be lived so much so that lived theology is theology.

---

[49]Winner, *Dangers of Christian Practice*, 5, 16, 79, 84.

CONCLUSION

I DON'T THINK I WILL EVER BE COMFORTABLE with systematic theologies. This is not to say that I don't read them, learn from them, and adjust my thinking about the Bible in light of them. I was reading Katherine Sonderegger's *Systematic Theology* as this book was in its final edits. I love it and get irritated by it at the same time. Her approach is worshipful, and she uses the Bible far more than many theologians I read. She challenges the framing of theology by Christocentrism in the Barthian mode and in its place opens with a big study of "the One God." Then she turns to this One God's omnipresence, omnipotence, and omniscience, and then moves to final things. Her second volume is about the Trinity, One God and Three-in-One or One-in-Three God. Frames matter, and systematic theology can be helped by reconsidering this sort of frame by mapping its frames more on the Bible's own frames—a narrative of some sort—instead of fitting various Bible verses or passages or authors into one's topics or the creed.

The most unnerving element of systematic theology for me is the rigid commitment to older exegetical conclusions. I respect that Bible scholars are actually shaped by older systematic constructions, but there are at times major leaps forward in our understanding of New Testament (and Old Testament) texts that have shaped older

systematics. I have often used the example of how *works* is understood so often in Augustinian, Lutheran, and Calvinistic perceptions
of how Judaism worked. That perception has been altered, which
means *works* and even anthropology shift in the doctrines of salvation in sometimes dramatic ways. With all due respect, keeping up
with the newest of the new is not needed, but major contributions—
such as Barclay on grace, N. T. Wright on story, and special studies
on the social context of the New Testament—have done serious
damage to older exegetical conclusions and should be given full play
in systematic theology.

If biblical scholars want to operate as doctors of the church, they
will need to respect the historic theological foundations found in the
creed, but respect requires engagement and even challenging some
points. If systematic theologians want to operate as doctors of the
church, they will need to engage paradigm-shifting contributions of
biblical scholars. I give one example now that I have not mentioned
but in passing so far. The Bible itself is a kind of history book in the
sense that it tells an interpreting history of Israel and the church. Why
do systematic theologians not have as one of their topics "history"?
Every day of every week pastors and professors and ordinary Christians are challenged to make sense of what is going on in the world
and in their local context. The creed and the topics might help, but
not the way a theology of history would.

We need each other, we systematicians and biblical scholars. Biblical theologians need to drop some of their testiness about the con-
ceptual clarities of later theological reflections, while systematicians
need to avoid some of their avoidance of fresh studies in biblical
studies. What we need now more than ever with the proliferation of
studies in both fields is regular opportunities to report on what is
happening in our fields. So I make this proposal: that each faculty,
and of course I'm thinking of seminaries but one need not think of
only seminaries, make a decision to make faculty meetings interesting

and informing. Hard to imagine, I know. What if in each faculty meeting a faculty member were asked to give a fifteen-minute presentation of new studies in their field, devoting the time to perhaps one major study or a fresh trend in studies?

If theology and biblical studies work more closely, and in doing so operate with a more narrative frame, a more historically sensitive and socially sensitive approach to what the Bible says in its context, and ask how God at work in history helps us to frame theology—if we do all these things, we will begin as well to make Jesus the person more central to theology. Sometimes I read theologians and Jesus seems absent. More often he has become an abstraction. That he was and is not. It was Jesus as a person who drew in the disciples, and it was encountering God that drew in those in ancient Israel from the patriarchs to the prophets. This form of teaching was not simply ideas but personal encounter, and we need to recognize the same in our own teaching. A lived theology that reflects the grace of God in Christ draws people to Jesus. God transforms by a radiating presence. One systematician, Katherine Sonderegger, offers this very observation in stunning words, so I quote her and reformat her words:

> But, we are drawn to a good teacher not by causes of some sort, certainly not by overwhelming cause, or external pressure, but rather by the teacher herself. Her instruction merely expresses what has already drawn us there, the being and character and wisdom of the good teacher.
>
> We are accustomed to speak of such power as *charisma*, the elixir of a remarkable human life. We do not trouble ourselves with measuring out the formula of such personal magic:
> so much learning,
> so much integrity,
> so much idiosyncrasy and freedom,
> so much danger or sensuous thrill.

Rather, the charismatic is a living whole, and we seek such a person, such a living power, from simple need. We come because we are drawn.

Mutatis mutandis, we can say that this is Christ's own reconciling and redeeming Life-Act, His very own Being, radiating to others. It is as though we are caught up in His own Life; we are assumed into this own Person, His blessed Intimacy with God, His own purely potent Consciousness of God. And we come individually but only because we are made a spiritual whole, a community of those drawn inside that Mediator. Just this is spiritual life, the goal of all creation.[1]

Since we are committed in the church to the scriptural revelation as the norming norm, we need to remind ourselves that our task ultimately is to conserve the gospel revealed in Christ by addressing our world in its local manifestation with the grace of God. We will discover that we each have something to say about that grace and for our world.

---

[1]Katherine Sonderegger, *Systematic Theology: The Doctrine of God* (Minneapolis: Fortress, 2015), 1:263.

BIBLIOGRAPHY

Augustine. *The Augustine Catechism: The Enchiridion on Faith, Hope, and Charity*. Translated by Bruce Harbert. Hyde Park, NY: New City Press, 2008.

Ayres, Lewis. *Nicaea and Its Legacy: An Approach to Fourth-Century Theology*. New York: Oxford University Press, 2004.

Bancroft, Emery H., and Ronald B. Mayers. *Elemental Theology: An Introductory Survey of Conservative Doctrine*. Rev. ed. Grand Rapids, MI: Kregel, 1996.

Barclay, John M. G. *Paul and the Gift*. Grand Rapids, MI: Eerdmans, 2015.

Bates, Matthew W. *The Birth of the Trinity*. Oxford: Oxford University Press, 2016.

————. *Gospel Allegiance*. Grand Rapids, MI: Brazos, 2019.

————. *The Hermeneutics of the Apostolic Proclamation: The Center of Paul's Method of Scriptural Interpretation*. Waco, TX: Baylor University Press, 2012.

————. *Salvation by Allegiance Alone: Rethinking Faith, Works, and the Gospel of Jesus the King*. Grand Rapids, MI: Baker Academic, 2017.

Bauckham, Richard. *Jesus and the God of Israel: God Crucified and Other Studies on the New Testament's Christology of Divine Identity*. Grand Rapids, MI: Eerdmans, 2008.

Bebbington, David W. *The Dominance of Evangelicalism: The Age of Spurgeon and Moody*. Downers Grove, IL: IVP Academic, 2005.

Beker, J. Christiaan. *Paul the Apostle: The Triumph of God in Life and Thought*. Philadelphia: Fortress, 1982.

Bird, Michael F. *Evangelical Theology: A Biblical and Systematic Introduction*. 2nd ed. Grand Rapids, MI: Zondervan, 2013.

Blaising, Craig Alan, and Darrell L. Bock. *Progressive Dispensationalism*. Grand Rapids, MI: Baker, 2000.

Bloesch, Donald G. *Essentials of Evangelical Theology*. 2 vols. Repr., Peabody, MA: Hendrickson, 2005.

Blomberg, Craig L. *A New Testament Theology*. Waco, TX: Baylor University Press, 2018.

Blount, Brian K. *Then the Whisper Put on Flesh: New Testament Ethics in an African American Context*. Nashville: Abingdon, 2001.

Bockmuehl, Markus. "Bible Versus Theology: Is 'Theological Interpretation' the Answer?" *Nova et Vetera* 9, no. 1 (2011): 27-47.

———. *Seeing the Word: Refocusing New Testament Study*. Studies in Theological Interpretation. Grand Rapids, MI: Baker Academic, 2006.

Boersma, Hans. *Sacramental Preaching: Sermons on the Hidden Presence of Christ*. Grand Rapids, MI: Baker Academic, 2016.

———. *Scripture as Real Presence: Sacramental Exegesis in the Early Church*. Grand Rapids, MI: Baker Academic, 2017.

———. *Violence, Hospitality, and the Cross: Reappropriating the Atonement Tradition*. Grand Rapids, MI: Baker Academic, 2004.

Bonhoeffer, Dietrich. *Discipleship*. Dietrich Bonhoeffer Works 4. Minneapolis: Fortress, 2001.

Borg, Marcus J. *Reading the Bible Again for the First Time: Taking the Bible Seriously but Not Literally*. Rev. ed. San Francisco: HarperSanFrancisco, 2002.

Boyd, Gregory A. *The Crucifixion of the Warrior God*. Minneapolis: Fortress, 2017.

Bray, Gerald L. "Grace." In *New Dictionary of Theology*, 2nd ed., edited by Martin Davie et al., 376-78. Downers Grove, IL: IVP Academic, 2016.

Calvin, John. *Institutes of the Christian Religion*. 2 vols. Translated by Ford Lewis Battles. Edited by John T. McNeill. Library of Christian Classics 20-21. Philadelphia: Westminster, 1960.

Campbell, Douglas A. "Apocalyptic Epistemology: The Sine Qua Non of Valid Pauline Interpretation." In *Paul and the Apocalyptic Imagination*, edited by Ben C. Blackwell, John K. Goodrich, and Jason Maston, 65-85. Minneapolis: Fortress, 2016.

———. *The Deliverance of God: An Apocalyptic Rereading of Justification in Paul*. Grand Rapids, MI: Eerdmans, 2013.

———. *Pauline Dogmatics: The Triumph of God's Love*. Grand Rapids, MI: Eerdmans, 2020.

———. *The Quest for Paul's Gospel*. London: T&T Clark, 2005.

Carson, D. A. "Systematic Theology and Biblical Theology." In *New Dictionary of Biblical Theology*, edited by T. Desmond Alexander and Brian S. Rosner, 89-104. Downers Grove, IL: InterVarsity Press, 2000.

Certeau, Michel de. *The Practice of Everyday Life*. Translated by Steven Rendall. Berkeley: University of California Press, 1984.

Chafer, Lewis Sperry. *Systematic Theology*. 4 vols. Repr., Grand Rapids, MI: Kregel, 1993.

Coakley, Sarah. *God, Sexuality, and the Self: An Essay "On The Trinity."* Cambridge: Cambridge University Press, 2013.

Creegan, Nicola Hoggard. "The Winnowing and Hallowing of Doctrine: Extending the Program of the Father of Modern Theology?" In *Sarah Coakley and the Future of Systematic Theology*, edited by Janice McRandal, 115-37. Minneapolis: Fortress, 2016.

Croasmun, Matthew. *The Emergence of Sin: The Cosmic Tyrant in Romans*. New York: Oxford University Press, 2017.

Croy, N. Clayton. *Prima Scriptura: An Introduction to New Testament Interpretation*. Grand Rapids, MI: Baker Academic, 2011.

DeYoung, Kevin. *Grace Defined and Defended: What a Four-Hundred-Year-Old Confession Teaches Us About Sin, Salvation, and the Sovereignty of God*. Wheaton, IL: Crossway, 2019.

———. "Those Tricksy Biblicists." Gospel Coalition. September 1, 2011. www.thegospel coalition.org/blogs/kevin-deyoung/those-tricksy-biblicists/.

Dunn, James D. G. *Christology in the Making: A New Testament into the Origins of the Doctrine of the Incarnation*. 2nd ed. Philadelphia: Westminster John Knox, 1989.

———. *Did the First Christians Worship Jesus? The New Testament Evidence*. Louisville, KY: Westminster John Knox, 2010.

———. *The Partings of the Ways: Between Christianity and Judaism and Their Significance for the Character of Christianity*. Philadelphia: Trinity Press International, 1991.

———. *The Theology of Paul the Apostle*. Grand Rapids, MI: Eerdmans, 1998.

———. *Unity and Diversity in the New Testament: An Inquiry into the Character of Earliest Christianity*. 3rd ed. London: SCM Press, 2006.

Eastman, Susan Grove. *Paul and the Person: Reframing Paul's Anthropology*. Grand Rapids, MI: Eerdmans, 2017.

Emanuel, Sarah. *Humor, Resistance, and Jewish Cultural Persistence in the Book of Revelation: Roasting Rome*. New York: Cambridge University Press, 2020.

Epstein, Joseph. *Once More Around the Block: Familiar Essays*. New York: Norton, 1987.

Fee, Gordon. *God's Empowering Presence: The Holy Spirit in the Letters of Paul*. Peabody, MA: Hendrickson, 1994.

Finger, Reta Halteman. *Roman House Churches for Today: A Practical Guide for Small Groups*. Grand Rapids, MI: Eerdmans, 2007.

Fishbane, Michael. *Biblical Interpretation in Ancient Israel*. Oxford: Clarendon, 1985.

Fitzmyer, J. A. *Romans*. Anchor Yale Bible Commentary 33. New Haven, CT: Yale University Press, 2007.

Frame, John M. "Is Biblicism Impossible? A Review Article." *Reformed Faith & Practice* 1, no. 2 (2016). https://journal.rts.edu/article/is-biblicism-impossible-a-review-article/.

Gaventa, Beverly. *When in Romans: An Invitation to Linger with the Gospel According to Paul*. Grand Rapids, MI: Baker Academic, 2018.

Girard, Rene. *I See Satan Fall Like Lightning*. Translated by James G. Williams. Maryknoll, NY: Orbis, 2001.

Gordley, Matthew E. *The Colossian Hymn in Context: An Exegesis in Light of Jewish and Greco-Roman Hymnic and Epistolary Conventions*. Wissenschaftliche Untersuchungen zum Neuen Testament 2/228. Tübingen: Mohr Siebeck, 2007.

———. *New Testament Christological Hymns: Exploring Texts, Contexts, and Significance.* Downers Grove, IL: IVP Academic, 2018.

———. *Teaching Through Song in Antiquity: Didactic Hymnody Among Greeks, Romans, Jews, and Christians.* Wissenschaftliche Untersuchungen zum Neuen Testament 2/302. Tübingen: Mohr Siebeck, 2011.

Gordon, Bruce. *John Calvin's Institutes of the Christian Religion: A Biography.* Lives of Great Religious Books. Princeton, NJ: Princeton University Press, 2016.

Gorman, Michael J. *Becoming the Gospel: Paul, Participation, and Mission.* Grand Rapids, MI: Eerdmans, 2015.

———. *Elements of Biblical Exegesis.* Rev. ed. Grand Rapids, MI: Baker Academic, 2010.

Green, J. B. "Narrative Theology." In *Dictionary for Theological Interpretation of the Bible,* edited by Kevin J. Vanhoozer, 531-33. Grand Rapids, MI: Baker Academic, 2005.

Grieb, A. Katherine. *The Story of Romans: A Narrative Defense of God's Righteousness.* Louisville, KY: Westminster John Knox, 2002.

Grudem, Wayne A. *Politics—According to the Bible: A Comprehensive Resource for Understanding Modern Political Issues in Light of Scripture.* Grand Rapids, MI: Zondervan Academic, 2010.

Gutiérrez, Gustavo. *A Theology of Liberation: History, Politics, and Salvation.* Rev. ed. Maryknoll, NY: Orbis Books, 1988.

———. *We Drink from Our Own Wells: The Spiritual Journey of a People.* Maryknoll, NY: Orbis Books, 2010.

Harris, Brian. "What Do Theologians Do?" January 8, 2019. https://brianharrisauthor.com/what-do-theologians-do/.

Harvey, Lincoln. *Jesus in the Trinity: A Beginner's Guide to the Theology of Robert Jenson.* London: SCM Press, 2020.

Hays, Richard B. *The Moral Vision of the New Testament: Community, Cross, New Creation; A Contemporary Introduction to New Testament Ethics.* San Francisco: HarperOne, 1996.

Henry, Carl F. H. *God, Revelation and Authority.* 2nd ed. 6 vols. Wheaton, IL: Crossway, 1999.

Hill, Graham. *GlobalChurch: Reshaping Our Conversations, Renewing Our Mission, Revitalizing Our Churches.* Downers Grove, IL: IVP Academic, 2016.

Hill, Wesley. *Paul and the Trinity: Persons, Relations, and the Pauline Letters.* Grand Rapids, MI: Eerdmans, 2015.

Hirsch, Alan, and Michael Frost. *The Shaping of Things to Come: Innovation and Mission for the Twenty-First-Century Church.* Rev. ed. Grand Rapids, MI: Baker Books, 2013.

Hodge, Charles. *Systematic Theology.* 3 vols. Grand Rapids, MI: Eerdmans, 1960.

Hoklotubbe, T. Christopher. *Civilized Piety: The Rhetoric of Pietas in the Pastoral Epistles and the Roman Empire.* Waco, TX: Baylor University Press, 2017.

Holcomb, Justin. "What Is Grace?" Christianity.com. www.christianity.com/theology/what-is-grace.html.

Horrell, David G. *Solidarity and Difference: A Contemporary Reading of Paul's Ethics.* 2nd ed. London: Bloomsbury T&T Clark, 2015.

Hughes, Kyle R. *How the Spirit Became God: The Mosaic of Early Christian Pneumatology.* Eugene, OR: Cascade, 2020.

———. *The Trinitarian Testimony of the Spirit: Prosopological Exegesis and the Development of Pre-Nicene Pneumatology.* Supplements to Vigiliae Christianae 147. Leiden: Brill, 2018.

Hughes, Richard T. *Reviving the Ancient Faith: The Story of Churches of Christ in America.* 2nd ed. Abilene, TX: Abilene Christian University Press, 2008.

Hurtado, Larry W. *Ancient Jewish Monotheism and Early Christian Jesus-Devotion: The Context and Character of Christological Faith.* Waco, TX: Baylor University Press, 2017.

———. *At the Origins of Christian Worship: The Context and Character of Earliest Christian Devotion.* Grand Rapids, MI: Eerdmans, 1999.

———. *God in New Testament Theology.* Nashville: Abingdon, 2010.

———. *Honoring the Son: Jesus in Earliest Christian Devotional Practice.* Bellingham, WA: Lexham, 2018.

———. *How on Earth Did Jesus Become a God? Historical Questions about Earliest Devotion to Jesus.* Grand Rapids, MI: Eerdmans, 2005.

———. *Lord Jesus Christ: Devotion to Jesus in Earliest Christianity.* Grand Rapids, MI: Eerdmans, 2003.

———. *One God, One Lord.* 3rd ed. New York: Bloomsbury T&T Clark, 2015.

Jacobs, Alan. *Looking Before and After: Testimony and the Christian Life.* Stob Lectures. Grand Rapids, MI: Eerdmans, 2008.

———. *A Theology of Reading: The Hermeneutics of Love.* Boulder, CO: Westview, 2001.

Jenson, Robert W. *Systematic Theology.* 2 vols. New York: Oxford University Press, 1997.

Jewett, Robert. *Romans: A Commentary.* Hermeneia. Minneapolis: Fortress, 2007.

Jones, Beth Felker. *Practicing Christian Doctrine: An Introduction to Thinking and Living Theologically.* Grand Rapids, MI: Baker Academic, 2014.

Käsemann, Ernst. *Commentary on Romans.* Grand Rapids, MI: Eerdmans, 1980.

Keener, Craig S. *The Mind of the Spirit: Paul's Approach to Transformed Thinking.* Grand Rapids, MI: Baker Academic, 2016.

Lampe, Peter. *From Paul to Valentinus: Christians at Rome in the First Two Centuries.* Translated by Michael Steinhauser. Edited by Marshall D. Johnson. Minneapolis: Fortress, 2003.

Lancaster, Sarah Heaner. *Romans.* Belief: A Theological Commentary on the Bible. Louisville, KY: Westminster John Knox, 2015.

Levison, John R. *Boundless God: The Spirit According to the Old Testament.* Grand Rapids, MI: Baker Academic, 2020.

———. *Filled with the Spirit.* Grand Rapids, MI: Eerdmans, 2009.

———. *The Holy Spirit Before Christianity.* Waco, TX: Baylor University Press, 2019.

———. *Inspired: The Holy Spirit and the Mind of Faith*. Grand Rapids, MI: Eerdmans, 2013.

Lubac, Henri de. *Christian Faith: An Essay on the Structure of the Apostles' Creed*. Translated by Brother Richard Arnandez. San Francisco: Ignatius, 1986.

MacIntyre, Alasdair. *After Virtue: A Study in Moral Theory*. 3rd ed. Notre Dame, IN: University of Notre Dame Press, 2007.

Marsh, Charles, Peter Slade, and Sarah Azaransky, eds. *Lived Theology: New Perspectives on Method, Style, and Pedagogy*. New York: Oxford University Press, 2016.

Marshall, I. Howard, with contributions from Kevin J. Vanhoozer and Stanley E. Porter. *Beyond the Bible: Moving from Scripture to Theology*. Grand Rapids, MI: Baker Academic, 2004.

Martin, Dale B. *Pedagogy of the Bible: An Analysis and Proposal*. Louisville: Westminster John Knox, 2008.

McClendon, James W., Jr. *Systematic Theology*. Rev. ed. 3 vols. Waco, TX: Baylor University Press, 2012.

McGrath, James F. *The Only True God: Early Christian Monotheism in Its Jewish Context*. Champaign: University of Illinois Press, 2012.

McKnight, Scot. *The Blue Parakeet: Rethinking How You Read the Bible*. Rev. ed. Grand Rapids, MI: Zondervan, 2016.

———. *A Community Called Atonement*. Nashville: Abingdon, 2007.

———. *The King Jesus Gospel: The Original Good News Revisited*. 2nd ed. Grand Rapids, MI: Zondervan, 2015.

———. *Kingdom Conspiracy: Returning to the Radical Mission of the Local Church*. Grand Rapids, MI: Brazos, 2014.

———. *Reading Romans Backwards: A Gospel of Peace in the Midst of Empire*. Waco, TX: Baylor University Press, 2019.

McRandal, Janice, ed. *Sarah Coakley and the Future of Systematic Theology*. Minneapolis: Fortress, 2016.

Meeks, Wayne A. *The First Urban Christians: The Social World of the Apostle Paul*. 2nd ed. New Haven, CT: Yale University Press, 2003.

Middleton, J. Richard. *The Liberating Image: The Imago Dei in Genesis 1*. Grand Rapids, MI: Brazos, 2005.

Mikoski, Gordon. "Practices." In *The Dictionary of Scripture and Ethics*, edited by Joel B. Green et al., 613-17. Grand Rapids, MI: Baker Academic, 2011.

Minear, Paul S. *The Obedience of Faith: The Purposes of Paul in the Epistle to the Romans*. Studies in Biblical Theology 2.19. London: SCM Press, 1971.

Mitchel, Patrick. *The Message of Love: The Only Thing That Counts*. London: Inter-Varsity Press, 2019.

Morgan, Teresa. *Roman Faith and Christian Faith: Pistis and Fides in the Early Roman Empire and Early Churches*. New York: Oxford University Press, 2015.

Morris, Leon L. "The Theme of Romans." In *Apostolic History and the Gospel: Biblical and Historical Essays Presented to F. F. Bruce on His 60th Birthday*, edited by W. Ward Gasque and Ralph P. Martin, 249-63. Grand Rapids, MI: Eerdmans, 1970.

Moss, Ann. *Printed Commonplace-Books and the Structuring of Renaissance Thought*. New York: Clarendon, 1996.

Myers, Benjamin. "Exegetical Mysticism: Scripture, *Paideia*, and the Spiritual Senses." In *Sarah Coakley and the Future of Systematic Theology*, edited by Janice McRandal, 1-14. Minneapolis: Fortress, 2016.

Neder, Adam. *Theology as a Way of Life: On Teaching and Learning the Christian Life*. Grand Rapids, MI: Baker Academic, 2019.

Neill, Stephen, and N. T. Wright. *The Interpretation of the New Testament, 1861–1986*. New York: Oxford University Press, 1988.

Oakes, Peter. *Reading Romans in Pompeii: Paul's Letter at Ground Level*. Minneapolis: Fortress, 2009.

Oden, Thomas C. *Classic Christianity: A Systematic Theology*. New York: HarperOne, 2009.

Olson, Roger E. *Arminian Theology: Myths and Realities*. Downers Grove, IL: IVP Academic, 2006.

———. *The Journey of Modern Theology: From Reconstruction to Deconstruction*. Downers Grove, IL: IVP Academic, 2013.

Ortlund, Gavin. *Theological Retrieval for Evangelicals: Why We Need Our Past to Have a Future*. Wheaton, IL: Crossway, 2019.

Packer, J. I. *Knowing God*. 20th anniversary ed. Downers Grove, IL: InterVarsity Press, 1993.

Pedraja, Luis G. *Jesus Is My Uncle: Christology from a Hispanic Perspective*. Nashville: Abingdon, 1999.

Peterson, Eugene. *Eat This Book: A Conversation in the Art of Spiritual Reading*. Grand Rapids, MI: Baker, 2006.

Peterson, Ryan S. *Imago Dei as Human Identity*. Journal of Theological Interpretation Supplement 14. Winona Lake, IN: Eisenbrauns, 2016.

Pierce, Madison N. *Divine Discourse in the Epistle to the Hebrews: The Recontextualization of Spoken Quotations of Scripture*. Society for New Testament Studies Monograph Series 178. New York: Cambridge University Press, 2020.

Rabens, Volker. *The Holy Spirit and Ethics in Paul: Transformation and Empowering for Religious-Ethical Life*. 2nd ed. Minneapolis: Fortress, 2014.

Romero, Robert Chao. *Brown Church: Five Centuries of Latina/o Social Justice, Theology, and Identity*. Downers Grove, IL: IVP Academic, 2020.

Rowe, C. Kavin. *One True Life: The Stoics and Early Christians as Rival Traditions*. New Haven, CT: Yale University Press, 2016.

Sanders, E. P. *Judaism: Practice and Belief, 63 BCE–66 CE*. Minneapolis: Fortress, 2016.

Schleiermacher, Friedrich. *Christian Faith: A New Translation and Critical Edition*. 2 vols. Translated by Edwina Lawler, Terrence N. Tice, and Catherine L. Kelsey. Edited by Terrence N. Tice and Catherine L. Kelsey. Louisville, KY: Westminster John Knox, 2016.

Scruton, Roger. *How to Be a Conservative*. London: Continuum, 2014.

———. *The Meaning of Conservatism*. 3rd ed. South Bend, IN: St. Augustine's Press, 2014.

Smith, Christian. *The Bible Made Impossible: Why Biblicism Is Not a Truly Evangelical Reading of Scripture*. Grand Rapids, MI: Brazos, 2011.

Sonderegger, Katherine. *Systematic Theology: The Doctrine of God*. Vol. 1. Minneapolis: Fortress, 2015.

Steinmetz, David. *Taking the Long View: Christian Theology in Historical Perspective*. New York: Oxford University Press, 2011.

Strong, Augustus. *Systematic Theology: A Compendium and Common-Place Book for the Use of Theological Students*. Philadelphia: Judson, 1907.

Swain, Scott R. *The God of the Gospel: Robert Jenson's Trinitarian Theology*. Downers Grove, IL: IVP Academic, 2013.

Támez, Elsa. *The Amnesty of Grace: Justification by Faith from a Latin American Perspective*. Translated by Sharon H. Ringe. Nashville: Abingdon, 1991.

———. *The Scandalous Message of James: Faith Without Works Is Dead*. Rev. ed. New York: Herder & Herder, 2002.

Thiselton, Anthony C. *New Horizons in Hermeneutics*. Grand Rapids, MI: Zondervan, 1992.

———. *The Thiselton Companion to Christian Theology*. Grand Rapids, MI: Eerdmans, 2015.

Trueman, Carl R. *The Creedal Imperative*. Wheaton, IL: Crossway, 2012.

Van Til, Cornelius. *Introduction to Systematic Theology: Prolegomena and the Doctrines of Revelation, Scripture, and God*. 2nd ed. Edited by William Edgar. Phillipsburg, NJ: P&R, 2007.

Vanhoozer, Kevin J. *Biblical Authority After Babel: Retrieving the Solas in the Spirit of Mere Protestant Christianity*. Grand Rapids, MI: Brazos, 2016.

———. *The Drama of Doctrine: A Canonical-Linguistic Approach to Christian Theology*. Louisville, KY: Westminster John Knox, 2005.

———. *Hearers and Doers: A Pastor's Guide to Making Disciples Through Scripture and Doctrine*. Bellingham, WA: Lexham, 2019.

Vanhoozer, Kevin J., and Daniel J. Treier. *Theology and the Mirror of Scripture: A Mere Evangelical Account*. Downers Grove, IL: IVP Academic, 2015.

Veeneman, Mary M. *Introducing Theological Method: A Survey of Contemporary Theologians and Approaches*. Grand Rapids, MI: Baker Academic, 2017.

Volf, Miroslav. *Exclusion and Embrace: A Theological Exploration of Identity, Otherness, and Reconciliation*. Rev. ed. Nashville: Abingdon, 2019.

Volf, Miroslav, and Matthew Croasmun. *For the Life of the World: Theology That Makes a Difference*. Grand Rapids, MI: Brazos, 2019.

Vos, Geerhardus. *Biblical Theology: Old and New Testaments*. Grand Rapids, MI: Eerdmans, 1948.

Walton, John H. *Genesis 1 as Ancient Cosmology*. Winona Lake, IN: Eisenbrauns, 2011.

Webb, William J. *Slaves, Women and Homosexuals: Exploring the Hermeneutics of Cultural Analysis*. Downers Grove, IL: InterVarsity Press, 2001.

Webb, William J., and Gordon K. Oeste. *Bloody, Brutal, and Barbaric? Wrestling with Troubling War Texts*. Downers Grove, IL: IVP Academic, 2019.

Webster, John. *The Culture of Theology*. Edited by Ivor J. Davidson and Alden C. McCray. Grand Rapids, MI: Baker Academic, 2019.

Weitzman, Steven. *Surviving Sacrilege: Cultural Persistence in Jewish Antiquity*. Cambridge, MA: Harvard University Press, 2005.

Werntz, Myles. "The Body and the Body of the Church: Coakley, Yoder, and the Imitation of Christ." In *Sarah Coakley and the Future of Systematic Theology*, edited by Janice McRandal, 99-114. Minneapolis: Fortress, 2016.

Williams, D. H. *Evangelicals and Tradition: The Formative Influence of the Early Church*. Grand Rapids, MI: Baker Academic, 2005.

Winner, Lauren F. *The Dangers of Christian Practice: On Wayward Gifts, Characteristic Damage, and Sin*. New Haven, CT: Yale University Press, 2018.

Witherington, Ben W., III. *New Testament Theology and Ethics*. Vol. 1. Downers Grove, IL: IVP Academic, 2016.

Wright, N. T. *History and Eschatology: Jesus and the Promise of Natural Theology*. Waco, TX: Baylor University Press, 2019.

———. *How God Became King: The Forgotten Story of the Gospels*. New York: HarperOne, 2012.

———. *Jesus and the Victory of God*. Christian Origins and the Question of God 2. Minneapolis: Fortress, 1996.

———. *Paul and His Recent Interpreters*. Minneapolis: Fortress, 2015.

———. *The Paul Debate: Critical Questions for Understanding the Apostle*. Waco, TX: Baylor University Press, 2015.

———. *Pauline Perspectives: Essays on Paul, 1978–2013*. Minneapolis: Fortress, 2013.

———. *What Saint Paul Really Said: Was Paul of Tarsus the Real Founder of Christianity?* Grand Rapids, MI: Eerdmans, 1997.

NAME INDEX

SCRIPTURE INDEX

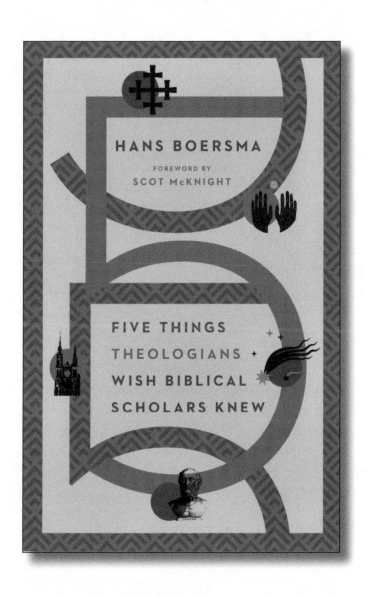

HANS BOERSMA

FOREWORD BY
SCOT McKNIGHT

FIVE THINGS
THEOLOGIANS +
WISH BIBLICAL
SCHOLARS KNEW